LORD
OF THE
FRIES

IT'S NOT ABOUT YOUR MONEY, IT'S ABOUT YOUR HEART.

DR. JEFFREY ALLEN LOVE

WHAT THEY'RE SAYING ABOUT
LORD OF THE FRIES

Jeff Love is one of the most creative and insightful pastors I know. In his typical fashion, he has taken a simple topic like "money" and expanded the teaching on the subject far beyond the typical pastoral perspective in *Lord of the Fries*. I know Jeff well and he sees things others can't see. It's a gift. And in applying this gift to Jesus' number one topic, he presents a truly moving case that brings conviction and compels you take action.

Bart Rendel
President & Co-Founder of Intentional Churches

I love it. The *Lord of the Fries*. This has my attention. I have known Pastor Jeff Love for many years now. I have seen him in many roles: a worship leader, an assistant pastor, a senior pastor, a painter, a lead teaching pastor, and now the author of two books. He has experience and wisdom. This book is important, this book is relevant and this book matters. It's about money. Money is a wonderful servant, terrible master. Jeff mentally paints a picture for us of how to use money...wisely. His advice: Don't make the treasure your pleasure. Make the Treasurer your pleasure.

Dr. Ed Delph
Founder and President of Nationstrategy

If you're a pastor or church leader struggling to teach your peeps the value of giving with a generous heart, then you've got to get this book! Jeff Love masterfully develops a casual conversation with the reader centering on one central Biblical theme - "Wherever your treasure is, there the desires of your heart will also be." And the practical information that follows is just priceless. I can't wait to give a copy out to my entire congregation!

Jim Phillips
Founding and Senior Pastor of
Life Point Community Church

The role our pastor fulfills in our lives is very important; almost as important as talking about money before and during your marriage. Dr. Jeffrey Allen Love is a gifted communicator of what God wants us to know from His Word and when it comes to our finances, he explains very well how one of our most emotionally loaded topics can impact our lives for the better. Take the time to read and reread the message included in these pages and know that you are loved!

Johnny and Stacey Stone
Afternoon Host and Co-host at
Family Life Radio Network

Jeff is an incredible painter but this time instead of paint and canvas he uses the artistry of storytelling through a simple metaphor to convey one of the great principles of God. You will enjoy the read and be challenged to get the optimal out of what God has asked us to manage. *Lord of the Fries* is a must read for understanding the responsibilities and blessings that God has entrusted to us.

Andrew Statezny
CDF Capital Leadership Coach and Multisite Expert
Bayside Church in Northern California

Lord of the Fries reminds me how often I'm guilty of believing that my stuff is MY stuff even though I know in my mind that it really all belongs to God. Jeff Love teaches important truths about our need to remember why money matters to God, and he does so with humor and personal stories that invite you to enjoy the read and embrace the message. So read, enjoy, and remember who really is the *Lord of the Fries*!

Steve Tanner
Senior Producer, Intentional Living Radio Program

Dr. Jeffrey Allen Love has put together a compelling description of what it looks like to TRULY place your trust in God. Trust is a topic beaten around by many, but fully embraced by so few. Through personal examples and wisdom built through years of ministry and just...life, Jeff provides a pathway for those willing to take it. This is not a book merely about finances, but a book that takes a 30,000 foot view of the totality of where your confidence will lie. After working alongside Jeff and watching him in action, I trust his perspective gained through his years of ministry and life experience. What Jeff has shared here has the potential to transform your future. I encourage you to take these spiritual strategies to heart and put them into play in your life.

Lee Coates
Executive Pastor, Ministry and Media
The Crossing Church Las Vegas
Intentional Churches Coach

Lord of the Fries

Copyright © 2016 by Dr. Jeffrey Allen Love

All rights reserved.

2911 Publishing

Printed in the United States of America

www.lordofthefriesbook.com

www.lifepalette.com

Edited by Julie Joiner and Jim Joiner

Cover design by Dory Gajda

Typesetting by Jim Joiner

Printing by Arizona Lithographers, Laura Davis

ISBN: 978-0-9969203-7-7 (print)

ISBN: 978-0-9969203-8-4 (eBook)

DEDICATION

This book is dedicated to my late step-father, Dr. Alton B. Tomlin, Ph.D. This past year Alton went to be with Jesus after suffering for many years from Parkinson's disease. This book is all about the heart of the Father for His children. I've known no one who understood the heart of our loving Heavenly Father more than Alton. Through all the pain and suffering, he remained faithful to proclaim God's praise until the very end. He prayed over me a few weeks before he took his last breath; his prayer was that all of my work and the work of our church, Alive Church, would continue to lead many people to Jesus and a right relationship with the Father. I dedicate the writing and publishing of *Lord Of The Fries* to Alton in hopes that this work will do just that in the lives of many.

TABLE OF CONTENTS

INTRODUCTION

Why a book entitled Lord of the fries? Already as you read to this point you may be asking yourself if this a book about money? The answer is no. Perhaps you may ask if this is a book about stewardship. The answer is no. Although, throughout this book I will use money as an example and talk a lot about being faithful in financial principles that God gives us for our good. It is the most tangible of all things when it comes to the point of this book, "Lord of the fries". In fact that is one of the main reasons that Jesus talked so often about money. Truth is though, this book is about the heart of the Father and how His greatest desire is that your heart would be like His. "For God so loved the world that he gave..." (John 3:16 NIV).

CHAPTER 1

I AM THE LORD OF THE FRIES

I love french fries. I'm not talking about liking fries; I mean to say that I am passionate about french fries. Even though they don't love me and are not good for me, I love them. Somehow, I have never outgrown the taste for fast food fries. In fact you could say I am a connoisseur of french fries. I've gone so far as to actually poll people in our church to discover new places to find the best french fries in our community. I've tried most recommendations, and still my favorite fries are McDonald's. They're about as good as you can get. But here's the deal, at my age I can't eat fries like I did when I was in my twenties. *(I could, I can, I've just made a choice not to based on my metabolism and doctor's advice.)* To keep myself in check I rarely buy my own fries when I go out to eat at a restaurant. Instead, I typically ask those I'm dining with if I can steal some of their fries. My staff and my family pretty much know if they order french fries I'm going to ask them if I can have a couple.

With most people I'm usually polite enough to ask, but with my kids it's different; I feel like I should be able to just take their fries. After all, I'm the one who paid for their fries. My kids are older now and they know the process so they've gotten used to it. However, when they were younger it was a different story. Often when we would go to a fast food restaurant and order their meal, it usually came with french fries. This was long before kid's meals came with healthy options. As children, when they saw dad

> *Hey, those are my fries!*

reaching across the table to take a few fries they would usually respond, "Hey, those are my fries." I was always surprised by that response. I couldn't believe my children didn't want to share their fries with me. After all, I'm their dad.

A LITTLE UNDERSTANDING

I was certain my kids weren't just being selfish and wanted to share their fries with me. They only needed a better understanding of the situation and how this french fry thing works with their dad. They needed to know that I am the lord of the fries. In other words, my young children needed to understand first of all: I was the one who bought them their french fries. Their mom probably would've chosen something different had she been with us. They needed to understand if it weren't for my choice and my ability to provide them with french fries they wouldn't even have french fries to eat at the moment. I'm the one who allowed them to have any french fries whatsoever; I dictated this in their life at that point in time. In fact I didn't have to allow them to eat french fries.

Second, I was much bigger and if I wanted I could physically take their fries from them and eat them all; I didn't have to share. There would be absolutely nothing they could do to stop me. After all I was a grown man, I outweighed them and was much stronger than they.

The third thing they needed to understand was I had resources beyond their understanding. In other words if I wanted I could go back to the counter and order my own fries. Actually I could bury them in french fries if I chose. As small children they had no money; they were unable to walk up to the counter and purchase french fries with a credit card and they couldn't even get to the fast food restaurant without me taking them there. Ultimately, I was the sole provider of their fries.

With all that in mind, had my children understood when I reached my hand across the table for a few of their fries, one would think they would be excited to share with their dad. I didn't need or want their fries. What I really wanted was for them to simply, out of love and understanding, trust me with their fries. I wanted them to know I was the provider of their french fries and, if I was going to take a few fries and they didn't have enough, they could trust me to provide more. I wanted them to be willing to share with me knowing how much I enjoyed the process of us sitting together sharing a meal with fries. My kids should have been grateful enough to willingly share with their dad without saying, "Those are my fries".

You see I didn't want to take all their fries, I just wanted a couple fries. I wanted them to be grateful, and understand I love them and I chose to allow them to eat french fries. I wanted them to share a few with me. More than just sharing them with me, I wanted them to want to share with me. Those few moments sitting in a restaurant eating french fries together was a special time for me.

OUR UNDERSTANDING OF OUR FATHER

Just like my kids, when it comes to everything we have, we need to understand our loving Heavenly Father provided it all. And in truth, if He wanted He could take everything; after all He's God, the Creator of the universe. Or, He could give us more than we ever dreamed. There's no limit to His resources. The Scriptures tell us that the earth is the Lord's and everything in it. The psalmist writes that He owns "*the cattle on a thousand hills*" (Psalms 50:9). Yet how often do we see ourselves pulling back our "french fries," telling Him those are "our fries" and to "leave them alone"? As though He needs our fries!

When it comes to being faithful with all God has given us, it's not that our loving Heavenly Father wants to take something from us; He wants us to willingly give what our money, our things and our possessions represent: our hearts. How crazy is it to think for a moment that God needs our money? That's like thinking I needed my children's french fries, as if they didn't share with me I would go without. It would be as if I would be lost without their generosity and couldn't come up with my own fries. No, I just wanted them to have thankful hearts and loving attitudes towards me as their dad.

Every day, like most of us, you probably get up, go to work and trade your time and skills, in fact your life, for money. You may push back on that thought; I know I do. I am so passionate about living my life mission and purpose I want to believe I would do my job for free if necessary. But truth be told, like most of you, if my employer could no longer pay me I'd eventually have to look for another job; I too need money to pay the bills and eat fries. There's nothing wrong with needing money; after all money comes in pretty handy here on earth. It's the system we have to provide for our children, to provide for our communities and to meet the needs of those in crisis around us. But when we are more consumed with money than we are with the love of our Heavenly Father, and when our hearts are bent toward pursuing the things of this world more than Him, it's a problem. The reason it's a problem, God wants nothing to stand between us and Him. He created us to have a love relationship with Him as sons and daughters. He wants us to trust Him so completely as our provider that He can direct us to take all He's given to be used wherever He wants to meet the needs of His kingdom and to carry out His plan.

The danger is money and all it can buy begins to possess our hearts. God, our provider, wants nothing and no one in possession of our hearts except Him. For the hearts He rules,

> *God wants nothing and no one in possession of our hearts except Him.*

He promises to provide for all their needs: "*And this same God who takes care of me will supply all your (my) needs from his glorious riches, which have been given to us (me) in Christ Jesus*" (Philippians 4:19). No one else and nothing else can make that promise and keep it. Money cannot make that promise, our homes or cars nor any of our material possessions can make that promise. Only God our loving Heavenly Father, through Christ Jesus, is able to make and keep that promise. Why? Because He is God; He does not need money or things. He owns it all and created it all. He can still create should He choose. What He wants from us is the one thing He's given us the power to choose – a loving relationship with Him as His children.

A NEW PERSPECTIVE

In Psalms 50:12 God tells the psalmist: *"If I were hungry, I would not tell you, for all the world is mine and everything in it."* From this perspective it seems ludicrous how we interact with God regarding our material possessions and money, especially knowing He's the One providing us with everything (all our fries). Think for a moment, who gives you the skills you need to do your work? Who gives you the breath you need to wake up and go to work? In the busyness of life and work we often forget this truth: He provides it all. He is the one who has given us the breath we need for life, as well as the skills and the opportunities we need to go out and earn a living. It is true He's given us our part; we are responsible to get up, go out and work every day – to be productive. However as you live in the discipline of developing your talents and using your skills, there is no guarantee of your next breath. Only God your loving Heavenly Father can provide all you need. Moreover, He is the one who has provided for our needs since the beginning of time.

As I wrote in the Introduction, this book is about us having the heart of the Father. It's about us being able to trust the Father with our past, present and future completely, spiritually, emotionally and physically. It's easy to get distracted with the "fries" in our lives. To think God is only concerned with what we do with all He has given us is like thinking the small fry is the super-sized. Don't get me wrong, He does care and gives us direction for how to handle all His blessings; we will discuss this in more detail in Chapter Eight. Be assured, He is more concerned about our hearts being aligned with His than anything else. A heart aligned with the Father's results in handling His provisions as He desires.

The truth is for most of us money is the last area we entrust to God. As a pastor for 32 plus years, I have to tell you I love teaching about the principle of stewardship from the Scripture. The reason is not because the church needs your money, and it's certainly not because God needs your money. No one reading this book makes enough money to out give God. And it is not because I need your money. Nothing could be further

> *The truth is for most of us money is the last area we entrust to God.*

from the truth, after all you are not my provider. The church is God's; and His church will survive whether you or I give money or not. The reason it excites me to teach these principles so much is that at the core of my being I'm an evangelist. I'm passionate about leading people to Jesus and making disciples.

It may surprise you, but when I teach about stewardship, especially when it comes to money, more people make decisions to follow Jesus for the very first time than during the teaching of any other topic. Why? Simple, this is the biggest issue standing between them and God. You may be even more surprised to know Jesus talked about money more than anything else, except the Kingdom of God. Throughout the Bible faith is addressed 246 times and love 733 times. Giving and our attitude toward possessions, on the other hand, are addressed more than 2,000 times. Sixty-six percent of Jesus' parables dealt with money and possessions. One in 10 verses in the Gospels, the first 4 books of the New Testament, do the same. Why is this topic mentioned so much more than a lot of topics we pastors spend much of our time teaching? Because generosity is an expression of faith and hope and love. It is the heart of our loving Heavenly Father: "*For God so loved the world that He gave...*"

A MATURE VIEW

Often we like the idea of God, learning His ways and living a better life, but truly being all in that's another story altogether. As a follower of Jesus we know this: at some point God is going to want to talk about your stuff – your money; because it is impossible to be a devoted follower of Jesus without fully devoting your money and possessions to Him. Still, there is a part of all of us, like children, that wants to say to God, "Hey those are my fries, leave them alone." We tend to lean toward the toddler mentality when it comes to the money and possessions God provides. If I have it in my hands, it's mine. If I have it first, it's mine. When I put it down, still mine. However, if I break it, it's yours!

As my children have grown older and matured, their status has changed a great deal. They have all come to understand when I reach across the table to grab a few french fries I just want their hearts. I don't want all their fries and I don't need them. I can buy my own. I can buy them more. I'm the one who bought theirs in the first place; I just want their hearts to be one of love and generosity toward me as their dad. Interestingly enough as maturing adults with jobs and the ability to buy their own french fries it makes a difference on how willing they are to share. My son is so great as a teenager; I often ask, "Joel, can I have a few fries? " He'll think about it for a moment and then answer, "Of course you can, you paid for them." Then there are those times when he pays for his own fries and he may make a different decision altogether.

When the tyranny of the urgent crashes into the priorities of our daily lives, we can easily be distracted and lose focus of this fact: God is God. He is the one who provides for all of our needs; He is the one who gives us life and the gifts and the talents we need to earn a living, and He provides us with opportunities. Throughout this book we will come back to these 3 simple truths over and over: He is the one who

> **God doesn't need our fries.**

provides all of our fries in the first place, He is God; He could take it all from us if He had it in mind to do so; and He doesn't need our fries because He lacks nothing. He could actually bury us in fries should He choose to do so. All He truly wants from us is what the fries represent, our hearts. He wants us to trust Him as our loving Heavenly Father, stand on

His promises, and live our lives according to His purpose and plan. As we trust He guarantees He will "*supply all of our needs according to his riches in Christ Jesus in heaven*" – all of our spiritual, emotional and physical needs. After all, while we may be the lord of our fries, He is the Lord of all. Knowing this we must wrestle with the question every devoted follower of Jesus has to wrestle with: Do we trust God as provider or do we trust money and possessions?

CHAPTER 2

OPEN HANDS...OPEN HEART

We ended the last chapter with this question: "Do we trust God as provider or do we trust money and possessions?" Let's work through this question for just a few minutes, because the truth is it brings tension into most of our lives. Before you read on I need to confess I'm writing from an area of strength. There are a lot of subjects I teach from a position of weakness, but this is not one of them. It's not that I have money or possessions, rather God has given me a strength to be able to trust Him as my provider. Don't get me wrong, I have plenty of areas of weakness God is working on and I'm growing in, as I continue to grow in this area of strength.

Here's the principle that helps give understanding to how we answer the "trust" question: whatever we open our hands to we're opening our hearts to. In other words, God has blessed us with possessions, money, time, influence and the list goes on. He has placed those things in our hands. Whatever or whoever we are willing to open our hands to, sharing those blessings, we also open our hearts to. I like to say it this way: Open hands...Open heart. Unfortunately the opposite is also true, whatever or whoever we close our hands to we also close our hearts to; this is the dark side of this principle. We get to choose to whom or what we open our hearts to. As stated in the first chapter, this book is about trusting God as our loving Heavenly Father – opening our hearts completely to Him.

A TEST OF TRUST

Prior to teaching on the subject of trust I drove past the billboard for our state lottery. On the billboard was an update of the potential winnings for the week. The number was a staggering amount: $300 million. As I read the number I felt the Lord question me, "Would you rather have $300 million in cash or trust Me to provide for your needs?" I took a few moments to prayerfully process the question. "Lord, are you asking me an either/or question? Either I have the $300 million and I no longer have You as my provider; or I have You as my provider but no $300 million?" Yeah, that's what He was asking. (By the way did you know that 95% of lottery winners are worse off financially 3 years after winning than before? And they are twice as likely to file bankruptcy as the average person.)

As I said earlier, trusting God as my provider, especially in the area of finances, has been a strength since I first became a follower of Jesus. (I'll tell you why in the next chapter.) But in that moment I paused and thought, "Three hundred million dollars is a lot of money." I'm not great at math, but I quickly did the figures in my head of how much I could spend every year of my life and still have plenty of money until the day I die. My mind began to think "no worries" for the rest of my life. I considered all the good I could do for God's kingdom, for my family, for our community and even for other churches and pastors. Then I was suddenly shaken from my thoughts; I realized I was considering a potential trade-in of God as my provider for money in the bank. It horrified me that I had even considered the thought. And even worse, the gap of time between getting the question and arriving at a solid answer defined my level of trust in God as my provider. It was only a few moments, a few

> *The gap of time defines your level of trust in God.*

miles of driving. But to think I would be tempted to even consider the thought revealed something in me that God wanted to work on. It was a test of this principle of living with "Open hands...Open heart" to God and God alone.

At this moment you may respond as I did when you consider the question: "Trust God as my provider or $300 million in the bank?" You may even justify it as I did, "Lord I wouldn't have to bother You the rest of my life; You could spend Your time and energy and resources helping other people and I would help You help those people with all the money I have." Seeing the gap between the question and the answer disturbed me a great deal, because as a follower of Jesus I want to be all in. Jesus said this in Matthew 6:24, "*No one can serve two masters. For you hate the one and love the other; or you will be devoted to one and despise the other. You cannot serve both God and money.*" It's either one or the other, not both.

FALSE PROMISES

The problem with money is it promises what only God can provide. Money promises security, peace and provision.

Moreover, the truth is we all have a longing in our hearts to experience those three things. In fact, it's a little taste of heaven to think of living in absolute security, complete peace, and never having to plan for provisions. While money promises these three things, it cannot deliver. Let me illustrate. One year my friend Tray's business was booming and he personally made $1 million. It changed his life; it changed his lifestyle. The next year Tray lost $1 million. I know what you're thinking, "If I had $1 million I would invest wisely and make it last." Most of us think we would never do the dumb things others do if we had that kind of money. But here's the point of Tray's story, money comes and goes. While it promises to give security, peace and provision, it cannot. Paul tells us in 1 Timothy 6:17, "*money is unreliable.*" Only God is reliable; He can provide for all your needs.

> *Money promises what only God can provide.*

God designed us with innate desires for security, peace and provision; He designed us to need Him and to trust Him as our security, our peace and our provider. He alone provides our physical, spiritual and emotional needs; no amount of money can cover all we need. Material possessions can't meet all our needs. No other person on earth can do for us what only God, our loving Heavenly Father, can do. And He loves to provide for us.

Is it God or $300 million for you? When your health begins to fail, which one would you rather depend on as your provider: money or the God of miracles and wonders? When you're struggling in your marriage or other significant relationships, which would you rather depend on: money or the one who has the power to change hearts and lives? If your children were rebelling and developing destructive behaviors, would you rather have money or a loving Heavenly Father who could reach out, guide and direct them to a right relationship with Him and to wholeness? Even more important, let me ask you in the words of Jesus: would you rather be devoted to money and despise God or be devoted to God and despise money? Hard questions, all of

> *Is it God or $300 million for you?*

them. The gap between the questions and the answer is trust. Am I trusting God as my loving Heavenly Father who provides for all my spiritual, emotional and physical needs? And how do I keep my heart open to trusting Him so completely? I open my hands to Him and acknowledge all I have is His. He is Lord of more than the fries; He is Lord of all.

How To Grow In Trust

Growing in trust seems like a mysterious, supernatural thing we have zero control over. And yet in Scripture Paul says: *"Teach those who are rich in this world not to be proud and not to trust in their money, which is so unreliable. Their trust should be in God, who richly gives us all we need for our enjoyment"* (1 Timothy 6:17). We are admonished to teach people to not trust in money but rather to trust in God. So trust is not really a mystery that just happens; it is an area in which we learn and grow. In the rest of this chapter I want to share three things we can do to grow in our trust of God as our provider,

LORD OF THE FRIES

so that we can live with "Open hands...open heart" toward Him.

1. Recognize the difference between wants and needs.

The first thing you can do to grow in your trust of God is to recognize the difference between wants and needs. Don't start thinking God doesn't want you to have what you want. When talking about prayer, Jesus said in Matthew 7:11, "*So if you sinful people know how to give good gifts to your children, how much more will your heavenly Father give good gifts to those who ask him.*" This verse is often taken out of context as if God would give you absolutely everything for which you've asked. Think of that concept from the perspective of a father. I am the father of four children; as they were growing up, while I wanted them to be happy and loved giving them what they wanted, there were some things I knew would be bad for them. For instance, when they first learned to ride a bike and wanted to ride in the street amongst traffic, the answer was no. Not because I didn't love them, rather because I love them too much to let them do things that could destroy their lives.

God enjoys giving us, as His children, things we want, things that make us happy. But He is a Father; and as our loving Heavenly Father, He cares more about our character than giving us everything we want. In His infinite wisdom there are times He says, "No". Don't be mistaken, God always answers prayer. It's just often we haven't learned to listen to and understand His answers, especially when He says "no" or "wait". Even when He answers "no" or "wait" we can trust Him to always provide for all our needs: "*And this same God who takes care of me will supply all your needs from his glorious* riches, which have been given to us in Christ Jesus" (Philippians 4:19). That is why it is so important to recognize the difference between wants and needs.

It is amazing to consider the truth of God as your provider. It's not as if He wakes up in the morning wondering about what your needs might be for that particular day. He knows your needs before you know them, He has seen them from the beginning of time. He is never surprised by your needs. You will never hear Him saying, "I didn't see that coming". It's not like He will get around to it someday or when He saves up enough. No, He supplies all of your needs from His *"glorious, unlimited resources"* (Ephesians 3:16). He has the provision waiting for you in the perfect time and place according to His perfect will for your life. *"Don't copy the behavior and customs of this world, but let God transform you into a new person by changing the way you think. Then you will learn to know God's will for you, which is good and pleasing and perfect"* (Romans 12:2). God is never late, never early, His timing is perfect according to His good, pleasing and perfect will for you.

The fact He has a good, pleasing and perfect will for your life is the reason it is so imperative you prayerfully recognize the difference between wants and needs. Know that He promises to always

> *Recognize the difference between wants and needs.*

provide for your needs and wants you to enjoy His provision in your life: *"Their trust should be in God, who richly gives us all we need for our enjoyment"* (1 Timothy 6:17).

2. Remember this is an act of worship.

When you open your hands to God it is an act of worship. This is why open hands lead to an open heart relationally with Him. This act of opening your hands to Him is recognition; He is the One who provided you with everything and you are trusting Him with all of your life, not just a part. God is looking for people He can trust with His resources. People He can depend on to move them where He needs them for the sake of advancing His kingdom. *"If you are faithful in little things, you will be faithful in large ones. But if you are dishonest in little things, you won't be honest with greater responsibilities. And if you are untrustworthy about worldly wealth, who will trust you with the true riches of heaven? And if you are not faithful with other people's things, why should you be trusted with things of your own?"* (Luke 16:10-12). Opening your hands to Him with all He has provided you is an act of worship; in which you are saying, "It's all Yours God, I choose to worship You, do as You wish with everything in my life".

The contrary is also true. In any area of your life you close your hands to God, you cling to something else as if to say, "It's mine, leave it alone". This then becomes a place in your life you withhold worship. It may not be intentional, but it is a barrier between you and your relationship with your Father; it is a withholding of worship. Jesus said in Matthew 6:21, *"Wherever your treasure is, there the desires of your heart will also be."* Notice: your heart follows your treasure. When you place the treasures of this world into His hands as a trusting act of worship, you open your heart to Him.

3. Return a portion to God.

In this section, I will not fully explore the process of returning a portion to God. We will walk through the practical process in another chapter. Here I just want to remind us again: all things come from Him, truly He is the Lord of the fries. Jesus confirmed this regarding His own life: "*Now they know that everything I have is a gift from you...*" (John 17:7). In context Jesus is proclaiming He is the creator of all things. When we acknowledge this truth, we understand everything is His and He can do what He wishes. We are simply looking for His guidance and direction. He directs us to live in the discipline of returning a portion, the first portion, to Him. Why? Open hands...open heart.

I can't help but picture myself reaching across the table at a fast food restaurant to take a few of my kids' french fries. I want them to joyfully and willingly allow me to take a few fries, knowing and trusting that I will make sure they have all the fries they need or want. In fact it is even better, before I reach, to hear these words, "Dad, do you want a few of my fries before I get started on them?" This requires knowing and trusting the heart of the father. It brings great joy to this dad's heart. It makes me want to provide for them in even greater ways, knowing they understand I am lord of the fries and want what's best for them; they can trust me with their fries.

Living out these three things will ensure continual growth in your trust of God and ultimately aid in assuring that you live with open hands and an open heart to Him as your Father. As you have seen throughout this chapter, God is not opposed to you having material goods, He simply does not want things to control you. Whatever or whoever you are clinging to with a closed fist, it has you. If you are not already, you will eventually become enslaved to the things you cling to and withhold from Him. That is the possession or person who has your heart. Not my words, but Jesus'. Read it again and let it sink in: *"Wherever your treasure is, there the desires of your heart will also be"* (Matthew 6:21).

Resolve that nothing and no one will have your heart but God alone. Resolve to live with open hands to Him so your heart will always remain open to Him. The more we understand this the more we understand why money matters to God. Remember it's not about a need He has, it's about how passionate He is about you as His child. In the next chapter, we will unpack this from His perspective.

CHAPTER 3

WHY MONEY MATTERS TO GOD

I have been amazed when traveling in third world countries to discover that the shed in my backyard housing my lawn mower is nicer than most of the homes of those living there. I'm not saying we shouldn't have sheds. After all, I have one in which to store stuff I don't need very often. One of my neighbors recently took on the task of building his own shed. It was nice, a lot nicer than mine. (Not that I care, a shed is a shed for me.) He spent many evening and weekend hours under the hot sun working on his shed. It was a thing of beauty. Then he fenced it in, along with his side yard on his corner lot.

A few months after completing this project, I was having one of those sleepless nights. In the quiet of the early morning I laid awake staring at the ceiling. So when a truck turned onto our road it captured my attention quickly. Not only did I hear it make the turn onto our road, but I noticed it sounded like the driver was taking off as if he were in a drag race at the racetrack. As he revved the engine and shifted through the gears, I could tell he was going especially fast for a neighborhood. Then it happened! I heard the sound of metal hitting metal and other sounds I couldn't quite distinguish.

I'm sure it only lasted a few seconds though it seemed the crashing went on for several moments.

I immediately jumped out of bed, got dressed and ran outside to see what had happened. The driver had lost control (if he ever actually had control because he was driving intoxicated), side swiped my next door neighbor's car, bounced across the road and hit another car, then hit a rock propelling him into the air through the neighbor's new fence and right into the middle of his new shed. Stuff from the shed was scattered everywhere. The truck was high-centered on the shed. The driver continued revving the engine trying to get away, but he was going nowhere.

All of the sacrifice and hard work: evening and weekend hours, the cost of building materials, as well as the value of the stuff stored in the shed; gone! In an instant. A quiet, unlikely neighborhood and house, not the typical target range for people going off the road, traumatized. My neighbor's blood sweat and tears spent in storing and protecting all his stuff ended in vain. As the fire and sheriff departments sorted it all out, and most of the nearby neighbors stood by and watched, I was reminded here was further proof our treasure is not here on earth. Yet, money matters to God. Why? Let me give you four very important reasons.

1. Money is a practical necessity.

> *Money is amoral.*

God cares about us, as His children, and since money is a matter of practical necessity here on earth, He then cares about money. Money is amoral, there is nothing moral or immoral about money. Paul wrote, "*For the love of money is at the root of all kinds of evil. And some people, craving money, have wandered from the faith and pierced themselves with many sorrows*" (1 Timothy 6:10). Notice it's not money that is evil, it's the love of money. So why does God care about it? Why is there so much talk about it in Scripture? While it's interesting how much God does talk about money and possessions, we humans don't like to talk about it.

I grew up being told never to discuss someone's income, debt or possessions. It was just plain rude. We are uncomfortable when someone talks about our money. What about when we attend church on the weekend and discover our pastor is going to give a talk or sermon about money? We wish we would have stayed home; there are a hundred other things we would rather be doing. Why is it such a personal matter? Because we have invested our time and energy to earn it, we have traded our life for money. And it's OK. We need to pay our bills, care for our families and eat; it's part of the world system we all live in. In fact, earning money is not in and of itself a bad thing. There is nowhere in Scripture that says so, quite the opposite: "*If a man will not work, he shall not eat*" (2 Thessalonians 3:10 NIV).

One of the most amazing things when it comes to our money and material possessions is the Scriptures often talk about them in reference to our spiritual growth. I find it funny since some of the best conversations I've had with people regarding spiritual issues are about money and possessions, even conversations with strangers. Deep down we need to talk about it, we may not want to but we need to, because we've given over much of our time and energy to making, spending and investing money. God cares about money because, while it is a necessity in this world system, He never wants us to put money or possessions before Him: "*But seek first his kingdom and his righteousness, and all these things will be given to you as well*" (Matthew 6:33 NIV). We are created and designed for Him to always be first in our lives. That is why He makes it clear: He alone is our provider. "*And this same God who takes care of me will supply all your needs from his glorious riches, which have been given to us in Christ Jesus*" (Philippians 4:19). It is so easy to forget He provides everything, including the skill and opportunity to earn the money we need to live and thrive.

2. Money is a matter of the heart.

God cares about money because it is a key indicator of the condition of our hearts. Jesus said it this way: "*Wherever your treasure is, there the desires of your heart will also be*" (Matthew 6:21). Your heart follows your treasure. Don't believe me? Think back for a moment about the interaction between me and my kids when it comes to fries. Remember I told you they feel a little different about me taking a few fries when they have purchased them with their own money. Now I'm not throwing my kids under the bus here; they simply do on a small scale what all of us do on a large scale. If we are homeowners, we feel a little different about our houses than we did when we rented; our hearts follow our treasure. If we invest in the stock market, we check to see how the stock is

> *Money is a key indicator of the condition of your heart.*

doing when otherwise we wouldn't care; our hearts follow our treasure. The scenarios go on and on, and we all begin to see how this truth Jesus talked about plays out in in our lives.

When Jesus talked about our hearts, He was describing that which comprises our mind, will and emotions. He was very clear our hearts, (our mind, will and emotion) will always be with our treasure. The question is what treasure do we allow to control our hearts? It's not always money, it could be a material possession such as a car or a home. It may be we've allowed a relationship with our spouse or kids to take first place, God's place, in our hearts. If our treasure is money, we will never feel like we have enough, regardless of how much we make or save. When the stock market is up we will feel up, when it's down we will feel down.

Just before telling us our hearts will be with our treasure, Jesus clearly contrasted the values of heaven and earth: "*Don't store up treasures here on earth, where moths eat them and rust destroys them, and where thieves break in and steal. Store your treasures in heaven, where moths and rust cannot destroy, and thieves do not break in and steal*" (Matthew 6:19-20). His challenge is for us to make certain our priorities are His priorities; our treasure should be things that do not fade, cannot be stolen or used up and will never wear out. In other words, heavenly treasure. Not that we will disown possessions, but that possessions will never own us – our hearts – they are reserved for Him and Him alone. There may be times when this means we need to let go of a possession when it begins to become too important in our lives. Jesus is clearly leading us into a lifestyle of contentment focused on the eternal and lasting treasure of heaven.

3. Money has eternal significance.

God cares about money; it is a matter of eternal significance because how we handle money is a test of our character: *"If you are faithful in little things, you will be faithful in large ones. But if you are dishonest in little things, you won't be honest with greater responsibilities. And if you are untrustworthy about worldly wealth, who will trust you with the true riches of heaven? And if you are not faithful with other people's things, why should you be trusted with things of your own?"* (Luke 16:10-12). How we handle our money on earth is a reflection of our trustworthiness. Jesus is clear: those who can be trusted with very little can also be trusted with much, but those who cannot be trusted with little cannot be trusted with more. This is something we all know intuitively but do not always practice.

For example, when a child asks to have a dog, parents may talk with their child about how they have handled responsibility up to that point in their life. It may be determined to get a goldfish first to test the willingness to be responsible for a pet. Not that there is anything wrong with goldfish as pets, but the commitment and needs of a goldfish are much different. Their daily needs are not as demanding as a dog's. If you are a business owner or in leadership you understand this principle completely, you don't give an employee greater responsibility until they have proven themselves with entry level responsibilities. If a person maintains integrity with the small things where less notice is taken, then they can be trusted with more responsibility. We must recognize here that the opposite is also true. If an employee is willing to cheat you out of $1, then they are more likely to cheat you out of thousands of dollars given the chance. This is an issue that goes to the very core of your being and surfaces in every situation.

When we recognize the truth that all our possessions and wealth, in fact all the world's wealth comes from God, then we will understand the importance of being faithful with all He has entrusted to us. Then we begin to have greater recognition of the need to be trustworthy in handling His property so He can trust us with the more important eternal possession of heaven. For all of the riches of heaven are of much greater worth than the wealth and possessions He has given us here on earth. Yet, this is the arena where integrity is tested and most easily challenged; the results of this test determine whether or not we are fit for the eternal riches of God's Kingdom. Money matters to God because He desires for each of us, as His children, to walk in integrity to succeed in preparation for eternity.

4. You have an enemy who wants you to serve money.

Remember Jesus' words in Luke 16:13, "*No one can serve two masters. For you will hate one and love the other, or be devoted to one and despise the other. You cannot serve both God and money.*" The enemy of your heart and soul, Satan, would love nothing more than to get you to serve money, to put money first before God. To trust in money as your provider rather than God is one of his primary tactics for drawing you away from God to himself. And Satan is so subtle about this, because none of us typically will make a decision to knowingly choose to serve him over God. Satan's strategy therefore is to get you to put something or someone before God,

> **Satan's strategy is to get you to put something or someone before God.**

knowing it is a choice that ultimately leads you away from serving and trusting God completely, and allowing Satan to have his way in your heart.

Jesus is clear here; there are two choices: God or money. It's one or the other. Please note and understand these are not my words; these are the words of the one who loves you and has a good and perfect plan for your life. These are the words of the one who created the universe. These are the words of the one who owns it all and promises to provide for all your needs. This is not a "both and" choice. This is "either or". If money is the master of your life, the one you serve, the one thing you put before God and do not trust Him with, then there is no room in your life for Him. As your loving Heavenly Father, He requires obedience and devotion, to be first and only: "*Seek the Kingdom of God above all else, and live righteously, and he will give you everything you need*" (Matthew 6:33).

A WARNING AGAINST BEING JUDGMENTAL.

This is a great place to give a quick warning about judging others. You see as a pastor over the years I have heard many Christians who do not have great earthly wealth judge those who do. You must know there are many rich people in this world who are faithful followers of Jesus, who serve God and

God alone. A person's net worth should never be a factor in determining the vitality of their faith. Jesus tells us in Luke 6:37a, "*Do not judge others, and you will not be judged.*" All of us, regardless of the amount, when we work, deserve to be paid: "*When people work, their wages are not a gift, but something they have earned*" (Romans 4:4). That is a normal healthy expectation here on earth and part of God's plan for now. The issue has nothing to do with money, how much you earn or save. The issue is this: for a follower of Jesus money is always a means of service. Money or accumulation is not the ultimate goal, it is simply a tool God has entrusted us with to do His work. And He trusts some with more than others because of their responsible stewardship. Know

> *A person's net worth should never be a factor in determining the vitality of their faith.*

this, money is not a measurement of your true worth; here we are all on equal ground, for each of us, in the eyes of God our loving Heavenly Father, are worth the cross of Christ.

MASTER MONEY, DON'T LET MONEY MASTER YOU.

No one wants to see their stuff destroyed by the neighborhood drunk driving through their shed. But we all know and recognize all our earthly possessions, including money, will one day disappear. God blesses us with possessions, great and small, on earth for our enjoyment. The danger is not that we have a shed full of stuff, but that the shed full of stuff has us. The constant battle of fighting against money mastering us can be exhausting. Unguarded, it can easily be allowed to take God's position in our hearts. God has given us a method for handling money as a safeguard to help us always make Him our master. A system (God runs the universe with systems) that works every time and guarantees, not only will we keep Him first, we will live with His blessing and provision. It is an ongoing choice and decision we must make. It is not a one time deal, but a perpetual working system He set in motion as sure as He set the planets in motion in our solar system. This system of keeping Him first and trusting Him as provider is always triggered by a choice He has empowered us to make at all times. In the next chapter we will unpack this incredible system God has put in place and how we can make sure we are enjoying the benefits everyday of our lives.

CHAPTER 4

MORE BLESSINGS THAN YOU CAN CONTAIN

When I first became a follower of Jesus as a teenager, I was blessed to have a pastor who taught me about God's financial system, and ultimately how to live financially successful. Reverend McAdams pastored a small church in a community close to my grandparents' farm where I grew up in Ohio. I made a decision to follow Jesus during a Sunday evening service at the church. On Tuesday evening of the following week, he drove out to the farm to give me some training tips on how to live this new life in Christ. I am forever grateful to him for taking the time and energy to invest in my life.

Reverend McAdams told me there were 3 things I needed to do to live successfully as a Jesus follower. First, I needed to read my Bible daily. He described how God had given us the Bible as an instruction manual for living and I needed it daily to grow in my relationship with God. Second, he talked to me about prayer. He gave me the low down on how prayer is the primary way to communicate with God and it too should be a part of my daily life. The third thing he talked to me about was tithing. While I had heard of the Bible and prayer prior to making the decision to follow Jesus, I don't recall ever having heard about tithing. Reverend McAdams described to me what tithing was and told me it was God's plan, God's system, for me to trust Him and put Him first in my finances. It was His plan to help me perpetually choose for Him to be my

> *Tithing is God's system for me to trust Him and put Him first.*

master rather than money. At the time, I had been bailing hay for my grandfather and some neighboring farmers, making a whopping $2.00 an hour. Reverend McAdams taught me tithing means the first 10% of my income belongs to God and He will bless the 90% for me to live on as I am faithful to tithe. I was new at this and Reverend McAdams showed me Scriptures explaining this to be the way the followers of Jesus obeyed with their money. So I began tithing. And God kept His Word, providing for all my needs and blessing the 90%.

You may be thinking it's wonderful that I was able to start my journey as a follower of Jesus in such a way, but for someone getting started later in life it's different. After all, you have a mortgage, kids to feed, college to think of, a car payment, insurance expenses and the list goes on. Even though I was blessed to begin my journey with the guidance of Reverend McAdams concerning God's plan and system for my finances, like you, I now deal with all of those same concerns. At one time or another most of us have struggled to make ends meet. Perhaps you have felt like the people of the Old Testament as God describes their financial scenario in Haggai 1:6: *"You have planted much but harvest little. You eat but are not satisfied. You drink but are still thirsty. You put on clothes but cannot keep warm. Your wages disappear as though you were putting them in pockets filled with holes!"* This may be your situation right now as you read this book. If so, as you put this principle into effect it will rock your world!

> *This principle will rock your world!*

GOD'S SYSTEM, YOUR CHOICE

As we saw in the last chapter, God operates by systems and this holds true financially as well. The great news about any system God has put in place is you can trust them to work, you can depend on His systems to always produce the desired results He has in mind. Just as sure as the solar system produces His desired results: We wake up every morning with an expectation the sun will rise and we go to bed at night believing the stars are going to come out. We expect the earth will continue rotating around the sun and as the year passes seasons change on cue. When the systems of your body are in good working order you are healthy. When one bodily system is not working your doctor says, "We've got a problem." Think about it, if you had to choose one physical system to work improperly in your body which would it be? If you are like me, none of them! I want them all to be in good working order; I want to be healthy! Equally as true, in order for you to be healthy financially you must depend on God's financial system to be in good working order, and it is. He's done His part and "supplies all of your needs." So what's the problem? His system of provision pivots on your trust in Him and the choice to obey the admonition to tithe. So, let's explore the concept of tithing a little deeper.

FIRST THINGS FIRST

The word tithe in Scripture simply means "a tenth". Throughout all of the counsel of God's Word, the Bible, He makes it clear His financial plan, His system, is based on giving Him the first 10% of all financial blessings He has provided you through your work. It's easy at this point to begin thinking, "But I earned it, it's mine!" Let me take you back to the title of this book and the illustration of asking my kids for a few of their french fries. I wanted my kids to remember with grateful hearts I'm the provider of all their fries and I'm just asking them to give me a few. I want them to remember that I can, if I want to, take all of their fries away from them; I'm much bigger than they are. I want them to remember that should I have a desire to do so, I could bury them in fries. I want them to remember that I am the lord of the fries.

> *God takes the responsibility and weight of provision off of my shoulders.*

Philippians 4:19 is one of my favorite verses, in fact it is one of the five verses I try to speak out loud every day: "*And this same God who takes care of me will supply all your needs from his glorious riches, which have been given to us in Christ Jesus.*" I like to personalize it when I speak it: "My God will supply all of my needs from His glorious riches in Christ Jesus." As I'm faithful to obey Him and do what He requires of me financially through tithing I know I can trust him to meet all my needs. He takes the responsibility and weight of provision off my shoulders, it is a place of freedom. He has proven Himself faithful repeatedly since the day I started following Him and Revered McAdams shared God's financial plan with me.

For a follower of Jesus the principle behind tithing is the most important principle of God's financial system: Giving to God first! Remember His desire is to be first in your heart and life. It's not that He needs or wants your money. He wants what it represents. The purpose of tithing is to teach you to always put God first: "*You must set aside a tithe of your crops — one-tenth of all the crops you harvest each year. Bring this tithe to the designated place of worship—the place the Lord your God chooses for his name to be honored—and eat it there in his presence. This applies to your tithes of grain, new wine, olive oil, and the firstborn males of your flocks and herds. Doing this will teach you always to fear the Lord your God*" (Deuteronomy 14:22-23).

When we start talking about tithe many people immediately begin to say, "Well that's Old Testament law." And actually with a little study you'll soon discover tithing began even before the law; again, it is a part of God's financial system. Going all the way back to Abraham in Genesis we see that Abraham recognized this principle long before the time of Moses and the law: "*Then Abram gave Melchizedek a tenth of all the goods he had recovered*" (Genesis 14:20b). While it is true you can find the foundational teaching about tithing in the Old Testament, the principle and system carries over to the New Testament. In fact, while condemning the Pharisees' neglect of the more important parts of the law: justice, mercy and faith, Jesus confirms tithing, it's the one thing they are doing that He applauds. *"What sorrow awaits you teachers of religious law and you Pharisees. Hypocrites! For you are careful to tithe even the tiniest income from your herb gardens, but you ignore the more important aspects of the law—justice, mercy, and faith. You should tithe, yes, but do not neglect the more important things"* (Matthew 23:23).

Everything about tithing points toward the principle of truly putting God first in all things. I have discovered throughout my years of ministry that for the majority of people who make a decision to put their faith in God, tithing tends to be the last area of struggle to put God first. I have also discovered when this final frontier of their faith is fully and completely submitted to God through His system of tithe, their faith grows exponentially. It always excites me when someone tells me they are going to put God first in their finances by being faithful to tithe. They usually report being scared as they begin this journey and ask me to please pray for them. I gladly tell them I will pray for them and I do. I share with them how excited I am to see how much they will grow in their faith.

WHY ALL THE EXCITEMENT?

Why am I so excited when someone commits to this step of faith? Is it because I am a pastor and know the church needs their money? No, you need to accept this truth: God does not need your money. I don't know of anyone in the world that makes so much money that God is cowering before them in hopes they will give a little to Him so He can do His work.

What an arrogant thought! The church does not need your money; I do not need your money. God is God and everything is His; the church is His and He provides for His church regardless of whether you decide to be faithful to Him in your finances or not. And as for me? Just because I am a pastor don't make the mistake of thinking the church is my provider. Just like you, God is my provider; I depend on Him and Him alone. Every pastor needs to remember this truth. Your board of trustees, elders, or congregation are not who you ever want to put your faith in as your provider, only God and God alone. So, why all the excitement? Let me give you several reasons I get excited as a pastor and why you should get excited as you begin this journey or continue on it.

God attaches one of the most amazing promises in the Bible to tithing: "*'Bring all the tithes into the storehouse so there will be enough food in my Temple. If you do,' says the Lord of Heaven's Armies, 'I will open the windows of heaven for you. I will pour out a blessing so great you won't have enough room to take it in! Try it! Put me to the test!'*" (Malachi 3:10). This is the only place in all Scripture where God tells you to put Him to the test. He promises as you do He will prove

> *God attaches a promise to tithing.*

Himself to you. He will prove He exists, He wants to bless you and He will provide for all your needs. It may be as you read this book you realize you have not even taken the first step of putting your faith in Jesus as His follower. You may not even be sure you are convinced that God exists. I would encourage you, no I dare you, to take the tithe challenge I talk about in chapter 12. As you do here's what I believe: God will reveal to you that He exists and He is longing to have a relationship with you. He will show you He desires to meet all your needs as you put your trust in Him.

Notice that He says: "*I will open the windows of heaven for you. I will pour out a blessing so great you won't have enough room to take it in!*" (Malachi 3:10). Don't think of blessings just from a fiduciary perspective, after all life is so much more than money. I know many people who have a great amount of money, who given the chance would trade it all for healthy relationships, bodies, families, fulfillment and other more meaningful blessings. While my wife, Kathy, and I have never had a lot of money, we would both tell you we have had more blessings in our lives than we have room for. We agreed when we were married we would continue on the path of putting God first in our finances through tithing regardless of our circumstances, we have and He has proved Himself to us daily. This book is not long enough to tell you all the stories, but let me share a simple one here.

Kathy loves to keep our home clean, and this was especially true when we had children crawling around on the carpet. She called me one day early in our marriage, we had two children under 5 at the time, and tearfully told me our vacuum had broken and we did not have money to replace it. She asked me to pray about it. Now I realize at this point many of you may be thinking God doesn't care about vacuum cleaners, and perhaps you are right; but I do know He cares about my wife and her desire to keep the carpet clean for our children. So we prayed about the need. The next day the UPS man delivered a brand-new vacuum to our home from someone who lived over a thousand miles away, someone we had not talked to and had no idea we prayed for a much needed vacuum. They just felt compelled the previous week to order a vacuum and have it sent to us as a blessing. God proves Himself when we are faithful to put Him first through tithing and we will discover more as we continue to read in Malachi 3.

In Malachi 3:11-12 God goes on to say: "*'Your crops will be abundant, for I will guard them from insects and disease. Your grapes will not fall from the vine before they are ripe,' says the Lord of Heaven's Armies. 'Then all nations will call you blessed, for your land will be such a delight,' says the Lord of Heaven's Armies.*" This is one of the ways He proves to you who He is. He is speaking here about your business. The people He is speaking to at the time would have understood this because agriculture was their business. For you and me He gives a clear picture that our business earnings will be blessed and protected as we are faithful to live in His system of finances through tithing.

There was a man in our church who, after hearing me talk on this topic, decided to test God by doing the opposite. He had been tithing and God had always provided. But he wanted to see what would happen if he quit tithing. He came to me after doing this experiment for 30 days and told me he had kept meticulous records during his test and discovered tithing truly made a difference in his life. You see, during the 30 day period he had unexpected breakdowns in his business, emergencies at home, several things that were out of the norm, all anomalies, that had become financial burdens. He said when he added up the expenses the total came to within

$1 of what he should have tithed during that 30 day period. He went on to say he could see that God no longer had a "guard" on his business, home and finances. He told me he had learned during this experiment when he put God first through tithing it resulted in God meeting all of his needs. God proved Himself to this man. He wants to prove Himself to us in a positive way if we will allow Him to through our faithfulness to tithe.

A REMINDER

I get excited for people as they commit to this journey because when you tithe it is a reminder to yourself every time you are paid that everything you have was given to you by God: "*But remember the Lord your God, for it is he who gives you the ability to produce wealth...*" (Deuteronomy 8:18 NIV). Rather than feeling like I'm giving God 10% of my money, I recognize that God is letting me keep 90% of His money. Without His help I wouldn't have anything. Think back to my fries illustration with my kids. It touches my heart, a great deal as a dad, when my children want to share with me all that I have given them. God teaches us through all of Scripture that His nature is to be generous. Think for a moment about how generous He has been with you. He has given you potential that is yet unrealized. He has given you gifts and talents to earn a living. His blessings have been dispersed in so many ways. His desire is for you, as His child, to be generous like Him. There are many other benefits you will experience as you are faithful to God's system of tithe, we are going to explore those more in the next chapter.

CHAPTER 5

HOW GIVING BENEFITS ME

The title of this chapter sounds somewhat hedonistic at first read. After all, shouldn't we give out of the kindness of our hearts? Of course we should be willing to give out of a heart of love remembering all the fries are God's anyway. However, it would be absolutely wrong to ignore the blessings our loving Heavenly Father desires to give to us when we operate from this core characteristic: "For God so loved the world that He gave..." (John 3:16 NIV). God loved; God gave. Giving is a natural response to love.

Jesus taught this is the more blessed way to live: "*It is more blessed to give than to receive*" (Acts 20:35c). Do you believe this, do you believe Jesus? The truth of Jesus reveals that the more blessed way to live is as a giver. Whether you want to be blessed or not, blessings are coming your way when you live as a giver. Perhaps you don't believe Jesus' statement. Let me illustrate it.

I love Christmas, not all the commercialization but the fact the world celebrates the birth of our Lord Jesus. I also love that we give gifts to one another as a way of celebrating God's incredible gift to us of making right our relationship with Him when He sent His Son Jesus to earth that first Christmas. When I was a child I couldn't wait to wake up on Christmas morning to see if I had received my favorite toy, the gift I longed for most of the year. But something happened as I grew older; I married and had children and everything changed. Suddenly those Christmas gifts under the tree didn't mean as much to me, rather I couldn't wait to see the joy my children had as they discovered their gifts. As a parent, it is much more joyful for me to give to my children than it is for me to receive a gift.

This is a truth Jesus knew full well, and willingly led the way by giving up His life for us on the cross. Why would He willingly do such a thing? Love? Yes, love and obedience to the Father, but there is more; He understood and lived in the knowledge of, "*It is more blessed to give than to receive*" (Acts 20:35c). In fact the Hebrews writer put it this way: "*Because of the joy awaiting him, he endured the cross, disregarding its shame*" (Hebrews 12:2b). What joy? The joy of knowing He was giving us a gift we could not give ourselves, a gift we could never earn, a gift only He could give. Joy awaited Him as He gave Himself on the cross because giving is the more blessed way to live. And He gave it all.

THE RIGHT WAY TO GIVE

> *There is a right and wrong way to give.*

There is a right and wrong way to give. When you give, the blessing God wants to give you can be stolen from you should you give in a wrong way. So what is the right way to give?

42

Cheerfully. "*You must each decide in your heart how much to give. And don't give reluctantly or in response to pressure. For God loves a person who gives cheerfully*" (2 Corinthians 9:7). Paul makes it very clear God doesn't just love a giver, He loves a cheerful giver. Back to my kids and the french fries: I don't want them to let me have a few fries only to hear them grumble and complain about it later. What I want is for them to have grateful hearts and be joyful because I gave them fries. What I want is for that joy to so fill them they can't wait to share their fries with me because of our relationship as father and child. I love it when they give cheerfully and it makes me want to bless them with even more fries, so to speak.

Not only are we to give cheerfully, but we are to give generously: "*Since you excel in so many ways—in your faith, your gifted speakers, your knowledge, your enthusiasm, and your love from us—I want you to excel also in this gracious act of giving*" (2 Corinthians 8:7). Look at the wording Paul uses; he wants us to excel at giving. To be generous. There is no greater generosity than that of Jesus giving His life on the cross. God excels at generosity and wants to see this same characteristic in us as His children.

Have you ever had someone give you something and then they complain about it? Or perhaps they held it over your head by reminding you of how generous they were to you, and you wondered if they wished they never gave it to you in the first place. Can you imagine God, your loving Heavenly Father, ever saying to the other members of the Trinity, Jesus the Son and the Holy Spirit, "Those humans are so wasteful of My gift of salvation, I wish I had never given it to them at all."

No way! It could never happen because His giving was born of love. The wrong way to give is out of obligation or begrudgingly. Giving is a heart issue.

Not too many years ago, I needed to sell a car Kathy and I owned. It was time to upgrade for two simple reasons: the mileage was too high for the distances we travel and the capacity of the car wasn't enough for all our children. I hate selling cars. It's just not my thing, period. Knowing this a former friend offered to sell it for me. We agreed I would pay him a percentage of the sale for his time and effort. He sold it for a fair price. I went to pay him his percentage and he wouldn't accept the money saying he just wanted to bless our family by selling the car for us. A few years later I received an email from this man complaining about the fact that he sold our car and I never paid him for his efforts. I immediately told him that I was sorry he felt I had done him wrong and I put a check in the mail to him for the amount we originally agreed upon and added in an appropriate amount of interest. The check was cashed, and I never heard another word from him.

Being a cheerful giver is a heart issue, it's not about just doing the right thing. Its about being so in love with your Heavenly Father, knowing and trusting Him as the provider of all your needs and genuinely understanding it is more blessed to give than to receive. It is clear that a truly joyful giver, a person who gives the right way, will be blessed.

BENEFITS OF BEING A CHEERFUL, GENEROUS GIVER

First, generosity is a choice that helps me be more like God. If you are a parent you understand; no parent wants their children to be selfish. Quite the opposite, we want our kids to be unselfish. God also desires unselfish children. As already stated at the beginning of this chapter, one of God's core characteristics is generosity. Scripture confirms this in many places: *"If you need wisdom, ask our generous God, and he will give it to you. He will not rebuke you for asking"* (James 1:5). So first and foremost when we begin to live as faithful,

> **Generosity is a choice that helps me be more like God.**

generous givers; we are more like our loving Heavenly Father; we are taking on one of His core characteristics. Remember God is not in need of our stuff or our money: *"Everything we have has come from you, and we give you only what you first gave us!"* (1 Chronicles 29:14b). All the fries are His to begin with; He wants our hearts and characters transformed to be more like Him.

Second, being a generous giver builds our faith. At some point, as followers of Jesus, each of us has to decide if we are going to trust God with our finances or not. Are we going to trust Him as our provider? In our economy we often look at things completely upside down from how God's economy works. Our economy says get, keep and hoard; the person with the most toys wins. In God's economy that's not how it works at all: *"Give, and you will receive"* (Luke 6:38a). He wants us to press in with generosity and He will generously provide for all of our needs. Paul goes so far as to say our giving is proof of our obedience to God: *"Your generosity to them and to all believers will prove that you are obedient to the Good News of Christ"* (2 Corinthians 9:13b).

A young man in my church called me one Saturday evening saying he needed to ask me a question. He laid it out for me: "Tomorrow I have a choice to make. I can pay my tithe but there will not be enough money left in my bank account to pay my mortgage, or I can hold back my tithe tomorrow and pay my mortgage next week." Then he asked the question: "What should I do?" Now you may be thinking this was simply a test for this young man and his wife who had two children to provide for, but don't miss the bigger issue; it was also a test for me. Was I going to remind him what God said in His Word and of His promises to bless when we obey, or tell him to think in terms of a worldly economy and go against God and His Word.

I responded to this young man by reminding him that he knew the Scriptures on tithing. He had heard me teach about tithing and generosity many times; he was on my leadership team and I knew him well. I could only tell him to do what God tells all of us to do, and that is to trust Him as our provider by putting Him first and tithe. I told him this was a time of testing. I asked, "Do you trust God; do you believe He will keep His word?" He replied, "I knew you would say that, but I just needed to hear it again."

The next day at church, he was there with his bride and his two young children. He did what he had been doing for a long time, he put God first and tithed. I prayed for him and his wife that God would not only prove Himself as their provider, but that their faith would grow. He did, and it did! The following week I received another phone call from him. Monday his boss called him into the office and gave him a position with greater responsibility and a raise; it was adequate for all their needs, including their house payment. A few weeks later he received a job offer more in alignment with his gifts and strengths and the pay was more than double his current income. He has told me many times since then he knows it all came down to that one moment when he had to decide whether or not he was going to step out in faith and trust God as his provider.

I'm not suggesting God will work the exact same way in every person's life. He is working uniquely in each of us as we obey and trust Him. Being faithful through generosity with all God has given us is an issue of trusting Him. Trusting, whether we admit it to ourselves or not, is one reason we struggle with generosity and money. As we are faithful to trust Him, it will benefit us greatly by building our faith.

> *Trusting is one reason we struggle with generosity and money.*

Third, giving is an antidote to materialism. As I said earlier in this book, God is not opposed to our having things; He simply does not want things to have us. He doesn't want His children to live in the bondage of materialism. He wants us to live in freedom in our relationship with Him. Materialism will lead us into bondage and choke the life out of our relationship with Him: "*No one can serve two masters. For you will hate one and love the other; you will be devoted to one and despise the other. You cannot serve both God and money*" (Matthew 6:24).

As a young man I watched materialism choke the life out of my uncle; he was called to be a pastor. He had been successful at a young age in business, then after making a decision to follow Jesus felt led to become a pastor. He quit his business and went back to school to get prepared. He became a pastor and was having success as he began serving full time in ministry. But soon, after missing the large corporate paycheck he began to do a business on the side. Eventually the business became more important than the church he pastored and he quit being a pastor. The sad truth is he was never successful in business again the rest of his life. And spiritually his relationship with Jesus went by the wayside. Eventually he left his wife for another woman and temporarily destroyed his relationship with his kids.

Now I'm not saying this will happen to you if you are materialistic. I'm not saying you should quit your business and go into the ministry; your business can be and should be your ministry if you are a business person and a follower of Jesus. I'm not saying that a pastor can't do both; I've known many who have done so quite successfully. I am saying materialism will destroy you. Don't mess with it. The moment you feel it's ugly grip, find your way out of it. Whatever is replacing God in your heart, make a decision to let it go. God cares more about you and your relationship with Him than He does about what you have or don't have.

> **Break the stronghold of materialism with generosity.**

When materialism has a stronghold, break it with generosity: "*Teach those who are rich in this world not to be proud and not to trust in their money, which is so unreliable. Their trust should be in God, who richly gives us all we need for our enjoyment*" (1 Timothy 6:17). By the way, the good news came at the end of his life;

my uncle realized he was on the wrong path and made a decision to completely give his life back to God before he died.

Fourth, giving will help us grow closer in our relationship to God. While materialism will choke out our spiritual lives, just the opposite of my uncle's story, generous giving will empower it. Why? Jesus gives us the answer: *"Wherever your treasure is, there the desires of your heart will also be"* (Matthew 6:21). Where is your heart? Money is like a magnet, our hearts are like steel, wherever we put our money our hearts will follow. Giving is an act of worship; it is a discipline in the spiritual realm that is like aerobics in the physical realm. It causes our faith and trust to grow with every generosity because the choice to give is made a new each time. The choice of whether or not we will obey Him, yield all to Him, ultimately is to remember all is His.

It makes sense that generous living draws me closer to Him when I understand and accept it is an act of worship. I am joining with God and His eternal plan by investing in others and the church. While it is true I can't take it with me, this is the one way I can send it on ahead. In

> *Giving is an act of worship.*

the New Testament Paul writes: *"Tell them to use their money to do good...share with others. By doing this they will be storing up their treasure as a good foundation for the future so that they may experience true life"* (1 Timothy 6:18-19). Notice the clarity Paul gives when it comes to using your money as an act of worship: 1) do good and 2) share with others, and by doing so you are *"storing up (your) treasure."* When you store your treasure with someone you will by default draw closer to them. Why? Your heart follows your treasure. Jesus said, *"Wherever your treasure is, there the desires of your heart will also be"* (Matthew 6:21). It's never the other way around, your treasure doesn't follow your heart; it is a discipline and an act of worship assuring your heart is in the right place.

The act of becoming a faithful percentage giver is key for perpetual spiritual growth – growing closer to God. The constant reminder that God's system of percentage giving through tithe, every time I receive a paycheck, increases my blessings and keeps me laser focused to trust Him as my provider. Doing so causes me to grow closer to Him and increases my faith and my desire to practice generosity with everything He has entrusted to me, accepting I am just a conduit of His gifts and blessings.

CAN I JUST NOT GIVE?

When I teach on the subject of tithe I am often asked by followers of Jesus, "Can I just not give?" I understand for many this question comes from years of bad habits which created a financial mess; and they may feel hopeless for not being financially faithful. The idea of beginning to actually live within a budget sounds painful; learning to let go and trust God first in your finances is a big step of faith. But the simple answer to the question is "no". If you are a follower of Jesus eventually God is going to want to have a conversation, ongoing conversation, regarding money. Because His passion and desire for you as His child is to provide for all of your needs and for you to trust Him completely. Jesus' words tell all: *"No one can serve two masters. For you will hate one and love the other; you will be devoted to one and despise the other. You cannot serve both God and money"* (Matthew 6:24).

God, our loving Heavenly Father created all the benefits that come with living a life of generosity; He wants us to live in the blessings of this lifestyle. The four benefits mentioned in this chapter are not an exhaustive list; we will discuss others throughout the book, although not in a list form. Another benefit is a principle God designed from which the entire universe is meant to operate, the more we understand it the more we will live in His blessing. We will dive into it in depth in the next chapter.

CHAPTER 6

SOWING AND REAPING

I mentioned my grandparents' farm in Ohio in chapter 4; our home was only about 100 yards from their farm house. Grandpa was a farmer. I learned a lot from him about life by watching him farm. One of the greatest lessons I saw in real life from my grandpa is found in Galatians 6:7-8, "*Do not be deceived: God cannot be mocked. A man reaps what he sows. The one who sows to please his sinful nature, from that nature will reap destruction; the one who sows to please the Spirit, from the Spirit will reap eternal life*" (NIV). You reap what you sow. Those words are often used when someone is doing something negative and rightly so. It's important though not to overlook that this principle God put into place, works for the positive as well. The crescendo Paul leads to in those verses is so incredibly positive for our lives: "*...the one who sows to please the Spirit, from the Spirit will reap eternal life.*"

As far back as I can remember my grandfather always planted just soybeans and field corn. Now this may be a shocker, but every time he planted corn an amazing thing happened; he harvested corn. Every time he planted soy beans, he harvested soy beans. Don't miss the power of this simple statement: he always reaped what he sowed. Never once did I hear him say he was shocked because he planted corn in a field and yet, the craziest thing happened, cotton grew in its place. It sounds silly, yet how many times have you seen someone, or perhaps you've been the one, who sows one thing in their life hoping to harvest something entirely different?

THREE TRUTHS ABOUT SOWING AND REAPING

1. You always reap what you sow.

Think for a moment of how this applies. What do you need? Whatever you need, you must first sow. Do you need friendship? Then sow into another person as a friend. If you need energy what should you do? You exercise, that is to say you sow energy. Do you need love and compassion? When you lash out at someone in anger, what kind of response do you normally receive? If you are reaping something in your life that is not pleasing to God or makes you unhappy, prayerfully consider what you are sowing.

> **Whatever you need, you must first sow.**

This principle applies to all areas of your life, including generosity. If you need money, what should you do? Give. The truth of this principle is, whatever you need you first must give. When it comes to our finances, the principle God's universe thrives upon, "sowing and reaping", applies. As I said at the end of the previous chapter, the more we understand this principle and put it into practice the more we will live from a place of blessing in all areas of our lives. Jesus wants all He is in and through us to overflow into the lives of others from a place of generosity. This includes being generous with the money which He has blessed us with through our work and otherwise.

2. You always reap more than you sow.

I watched my grandfather put one seed of corn in the soil and at harvest season he often reaped two ears of corn for each seed. (Warning: this works for anything negative you sow as well. If you sow criticism you may reap more criticism than you have sown. But let's continue to look at this principle in the way God intended: for positive results in our lives.)

To fully grasp this concept in relationship to your finances we need to unpack Jesus' words in Luke 6:38, "*Give, and you will receive. Your gift will return to you in full—pressed down, shaken together to make room for more, running over, and poured into your lap. The amount you give will determine the amount you get back.*" Notice the principle of sowing and reaping in His words: "*Give, and you will receive.*" Everything about receiving hinges on giving as a launch pad. My grandfather only expected to harvest from fields he planted seed in first. The base level of living this principle is found in God's financial system for us; we are to perpetually give back to Him through tithe and otherwise. This life

> *Generosity grows out of gratitude and trust.*

of extravagant generosity grows out of gratitude and trust. Much the same way I desire my kids to be grateful and trust me with their fries. To fully subscribe to the principle of sowing it is imperative you understand what Jesus said about reaping.

"Your gift will return to you in full—pressed down..."

Jesus tells us we will receive when we give. Let me give you a picture of what this looks like. I do not like clutter. In fact, I love to get rid of stuff. It's a little weird but I love trash day at our house. Hearing the trash truck stop and empty our trash can puts a smile on my face, just knowing the trash and junk I put in the can has left the premises. I hate to set my trash can out on the street only half full. I want the trash truck to remove as much trash, clutter and junk from my house as possible each time it comes. One of the ways I make sure this happens is by getting in the trash can and jumping up and down on the trash to compact it making room for more trash. Then I find more stuff to put in the can. I get more trash in my trash can than the average person because I make sure it is *"pressed down."* (Once my kids were old enough I gladly handed over the job of jumping up and down to compact trash.)

*"...shaken together
to make room for more..."*

I never quite understood this line until I married my wife Kathy. One of the things we love to do as a couple is going to the movie theater. Part of the experience is getting popcorn. (If you are like us, it's hard to go to the theater and smell popcorn in the air and not get popcorn.) Once we get the popcorn and are settled into our seats for the movie, Kathy will shake the popcorn bag to distribute the butter and salt I put on top through the rest of the popcorn. The unintended consequence of shaking the popcorn is the popcorn is compressed leaving "room for more" popcorn in the bag.

*"...running over,
and poured into your lap..."*

Have you ever been surprised at a restaurant when you received the check to discover you had been billed for all of the soda refills? I have and I learned my lesson to be sure and ask if refills were free before accepting them. This phrase is a picture of free refills, more than you can drink or contain. Notice once again the connection of those words specifically to God's financial system of giving to Him first through tithing: *"I will open the windows of heaven for you. I will pour out a blessing so great you won't have enough room to take it in!"* (Malachi 3:10b).

3. You sow in one season and reap in another.

Often when I teach about this principle at church, someone who began tithing or living in generosity one weekend will seek me out the next to tell me this principle is not working. When I inquire as to what they mean I am often met with a story of how they gave but had not received any increase in proportion to their giving. At that point I have to refer back to my grandfather and all I learned from him about this topic on the farm.

You see grandpa never put seed in the ground one day and then went back out to the field the next day in hopes the seed had already produced a harvest. He understood that once you sow seed there is a season of growing before the harvest.

During the season of growing he did his part through cultivation; that is to say, he made sure the seeds had the right environment to grow to full maturity. He would do this by fertilizing the soil, keeping the weeds out and making sure there was plenty of water. Although with most of what my grandfather planted He depended completely on God for the watering.

ATTITUDE TRUMPS AMOUNT

We did a campaign to construct our church building; we used the slogan "equal sacrifice not equal giving." I didn't coin the phrase and have no idea who did. But this is a powerful part of the principle of sowing and reaping. Often we think we don't make enough or have enough to give, yet God's financial system of tithing shows we all have the privilege of participating through giving the first 10%. I have people tell me that when they begin making a certain amount then they will begin to tithe. However, I have learned if you are not willing to be faithful to God with the first 10% of a dollar, you will struggle to be faithful with 10% of $100. If you are not faithful with 10% of $1,000 you will struggle with being faith with 10% of $10,000. You can see where this is leading. Actually the more income you have, the greater the potential struggle. The reason is we begin to drift from the purpose. The purpose is not that God or the church needs your money, it's that He wants what it represents – your heart. But with money, we tend to look at the amount rather than the heart issue. When we do, we may be so blessed that we have given such a great amount we feel

> God wants what money represents – your heart.

we don't need to give more. Nothing could be further from the truth. Giving is about an attitude of faithfulness and obedience to Him as the provider of all things.

At one point Jesus was with His disciples in the temple. He sat down on the opposite side of where the offerings were being given and watched the crowd gathered there. (Lest we think Jesus is not watching what we do with money this clearly illustrates He does.) *"Jesus sat down near the collection box in the Temple and watched as the crowds dropped in their money. Many rich people put in large amounts. Then a poor widow came and dropped in two small coins. Jesus called his disciples to him and said, 'I tell you the truth, this poor widow has given more than all the others who are making contributions. For they gave a tiny part of their surplus, but she, poor as she is, has given everything she had to live on'"* (Mark 12:41-44).

Clearly the rich in the crowd gave a greater amount of money than did this poor widow, yet Jesus was not looking at the amount but the attitude of sacrifice. This is a picture of why it is harder to remain faithful as we make more money, because we get comfortable and it no longer feels like a sacrifice. Yet God wants us to remain in an attitude of trust with this area of our lives remembering it is all His, always; and to never allow the grip of money or materialism to get between us and Him.

> *Sowing and reaping are perpetual.*

Every time we earn we have a decision to make: Are we going to continue to sow and trust God with our finances? Sowing and reaping are perpetual. Stop sowing and eventually you will stop reaping. Continue sowing and you will continue to reap a harvest.

It would be foolish to think I can opt out of God's financial system at any point in my life; and to hope He would be fine with this is more foolish. If I am going to live as a devoted follower of Jesus I will, at some point, have to deal with devoting my finances to Him and trust Him with it all. A farmer knows if he is to harvest he has to plant every year. In fact Paul shows us the more generous the farmer is in planting the seed the greater the harvest: *"Remember this—a farmer who plants only a few seeds will get a small crop. But the one who plants generously will get a generous crop. You must each decide in your heart how much to give"* (2 Corinthians 9:6-7a). You get to decide the size of your harvest based on what you choose to sow through your generosity. God makes it clear that the base line of His financial system is giving the first 10% back to Him in tithe. He tells us when we tithe He will *"pour out a blessing so great you won't have enough room to take it in!"* (Malachi 3:10).

| *You always reap more than you sow.* | Beyond the tithe we get a choice of how generous we will be in our giving; remembering to reap more you simply sow more. You decide. |

Offerings of generosity, sowing beyond the tithe, should be prayerfully considered to assure that you are following His leading. Paul continues in 2 Corinthians 9:7, *"And don't give reluctantly or in response to pressure. For God loves a person who gives cheerfully."* Paul instructs us that we are not to act impulsively or allow others to pressure us when it comes to giving; rather we are to prayerfully decide what God wants us to give. We must consider and assess our ability to live in generosity beyond the tithe we are called to and give accordingly. Everything about this is intentional and planned, just as a farmer is deliberate in sowing seed in a field for harvest. Paul had already sent out a challenge to live as a percentage giver: "*You should follow the same procedure I gave to the churches in Galatia. On the first day of each week, you should each put aside a portion of the money you have earned. Don't wait until I get there and then try to collect it all at once*" (1 Corinthians 16:1b-2).

The principle of sowing and reaping demands we do not give under pressure or coercion, but rather prayerfully and intentionally. God's primary concern is not with the amount we give; He is concerned with our hearts. He is not looking at the gift; He is working to make the giver more like Him. Therefore, individual obedience to the voice of the Father and His Spirit are the only promptings that should engage the believer in generosity. After all, remember it is all His, we are the caretakers of His assets. The more He sees He can trust us, the more He multiplies the harvest. He is looking for those who realize and understand the truth of His provision and willingly give faithfully with a grateful attitude for all He has given.

Generosity has absolutely nothing to do with the amount given. A person who only has a small gift to sow should never feel a sense of embarrassment. Attitude always trumps amount: "*God loves a person who gives cheerfully.*" God leads the way in

> *Generosity has nothing to do with the amount.*

giving. It pleases Him to give to us, the ones He has created in His image, with generosity and joy: "*And God will generously provide all you need. Then you will always have everything you need and plenty left over to share with others*" (2 Corinthians 9:8).

PREPARE FOR GOD'S BLESSING

As you live in the principle of sowing and reaping you should prepare for God's blessing. "*Give generously to the poor, not grudgingly, for the Lord your God will bless you in everything you do*" (Deuteronomy 15:10). Notice the writer says God will bless you in everything you do as you give generously, particularly to the poor. His blessings come so we can continue to live in generosity, so be prepared for any form of blessing He gives as you sow in generosity. I can't imagine any farmer planting seed – sowing – without an expectation of a harvest; I know my grandfather never did. To plant seed and not cultivate it, to have no expectation of a harvest, would be wasteful. God would surely trust the seed to another more faithful with His wealth.

My wife Kathy and I have seen this principle at work in our lives continuously, from simple things like keeping our washer going to much greater blessings in our relationships and more. We have remained faithful to sow, especially in tithe, putting Him first, trusting that He is our provider and He is the one who gives blessings for such fidelity. Let me close this chapter by sharing a story of how we have seen this work in our lives; it is one of many such experiences.

THE SHAMU MIRACLE

One summer we promised our kids we would take them to Sea World in San Diego, a short six hour drive from our home in the desert. Unfortunately, we had some financial emergencies arise we were not prepared for at the time. One of which, our car broke down and was unrepairable; we had no transportation for the trip. With that, all of the money for Sea World tickets, hotel and food was consumed. In chapter 9 we will cover weathering financial storms; but we all recognize we are not God and do not know the future; we can only prepare based on His direction, our limited knowledge and His provision.

Even though our budgeted trip money had been exhausted elsewhere, we believed God had led us to take this trip. So we continued to plan and talk about it with our kids, and Kathy and I prayed. Throughout this time we remained faithful to put God first in our finances through tithe, as we did we prepared for what He was going to do in blessings. Our family was a few weeks away from taking the trip, we still had no money, vehicle or place to stay. But we were preparing for God's blessing.

The week before we were to go, we saw a ministry that was doing a raffle to raise funds, one of the giveaways was 4 tickets to Sea World (we only had 2 children at the time). We knew those were our tickets. We entered the raffle and sure enough we were drawn. That same week a man called me who did not even attend our church; he asked if I could come and see him at his office. I did. He simply wanted to meet with me to tell me he felt the Lord had told him to give me a car. It was a big old 4 door Buick with only 40,000 miles on it, which our family aptly named Shamu. (Not only because of the trip but it was a whale of a car.) We took many great family trips in Shamu in the years to follow.

At the end of that same week I shared with our congregation we would be out of town the next week. I did not mention we were going on our trip even if we had to camp on the beach, which would have been fine with us. After the service a man from our congregation came up to me and said "I don't know if you would be interested or not, but my company has a condo in San Diego that I get to use one week a year. This year I'm not going to be able to use my week. Your family is welcome to use it this week if you would like." Would like? You bet!

Needless to say our family had an amazing trip, but even more important than the trip, for Kathy and I, had been the faith journey. As we continued to put God first in our finances our girls saw how God works when we are faithful to sow; it was more than we could ever have imagined. You reap what you sow. You always reap more than you sow. You sow in one season and reap in another. So be faithful to sow and then prepare to reap the blessings God has for you and your family. If you are waiting for a harvest but have not started sowing, begin to give. It may feel challenging, but as you will see in the next chapter through Dirk and Samantha's story you can do it!

CHAPTER 7

GETTING STARTED

Dirk and Samantha waited for the crowd to clear out after the service; I had spoken on the subject of generosity. I focused especially on the topic of trusting God completely by putting Him first in finances through tithing. They asked to talk with me for a few moments in private. We went to my office just off of the main auditorium in our building.

Tears rolled down their cheeks as they told their painful story. Although their story is a very common one in our culture, in their words it was "embarrassing". They proceeded to tell me about how they wanted to put God first in their finances but they just couldn't. They had allowed debt to rule their lives up until that point, so much so they were in the process of bankruptcy. They asked, "What do we do with what you just talked about? How do we trust God with our finances through tithing when we can't even pay our bills?" It is a legitimate question and it's one many people have after hearing a talk on tithing, or perhaps after reading this book. The answer I give is the same for everyone; it's really not my answer, it's God's answer: *"Bring all the tithes into the storehouse so there will be enough food in my Temple. If you do,' says the Lord of Heaven's Armies, 'I will open the windows of heaven for you. I will pour out a blessing so great you won't have enough room to take it in! Try it! Put me to the test!'"* (Malachi 3:10). I told them, "You have to get your finances into God's hands. In your hands it has brought you to bankruptcy and shame. Now you need to trust Him with your money and let Him begin to work in the mess you have created." They committed to do just that with a sense of trepidation, as they did God began to work miracles in their lives.

Often we feel the need to get some things in order, to fix the messes we've made before we can start giving to God. By the way, this is a natural response in every area of our lives. I can't even begin to tell you how many people I've invited to church over the years who responded with something like "I need to get my life cleaned up, then I'm going to get right with God." No, that's not how this works at all. If we could have done it on our own, we probably would have done it already. God's plan is that we come to Him and let Him get our lives in order through His power working in us. This is true in every area of our lives, including finances. We give our finances to Him by putting Him first through tithe, trusting Him as Lord of all. In chapter 9 we will address other Scriptural principles we need to put in place to live financially sound. Tithing is just the foundational step we need to take to trust Him with our money.

WHEN SHOULD I GET STARTED?

The time to get started trusting God with our money is often when we are in greatest need. This goes back to the concept of the previous chapter: Sowing and Reaping. The reason most of us have financial trouble is we have not been sowing our finances according to God's plan and in obedience with Him. I understand there are many circumstances where this is not true, for example a medical crisis that becomes a financial drain. Even then, perhaps most important then, we need to rely on God as the one who provides for all of our needs: "*And this same God who takes care of me will supply all your needs from his glorious riches, which have been given to us in Christ Jesus*" (Philippians 4:19).

When you need money the most, you may feel it's the hardest time to begin the journey of putting God first through tithing. The reason it feels so hard is faith is required. Faith is a muscle we have to exercise. You have to ask yourself; "Do I really believe God will do what He says He will do if I give

> *Trust God with your money when you need it most.*

Him the first 10%?" "*I will open the windows of heaven for you. I will pour out a blessing so great you won't have enough room to take it in! Try it! Put me to the test! Your crops will be abundant, for I will guard them from insects and disease. Your grapes will not fall from the vine before they are ripe,' says the Lord of Heaven's Armies*" (Malachi 3:10b-11). It may feel like you have to make the first move, but it is simply not true. God as your loving Heavenly Father made the first move through the cross and has committed to providing for all of your needs: spiritual, physical and emotional. You simply need to trust Him.

Notice in Malachi 3:10 God says "*Put me to the test!*" This is the only place in all of the Bible God gives permission for you to test Him. Put Him to the test; He promises to prove Himself true to you as you faithfully trust Him in this area of your life. The results are amazing:

"I will pour out a blessing so great
you won't have enough room to take it in!"

I have friends who hear my stories and tell me, "You are so lucky." I quickly respond with "No, I'm blessed." You see even though I made some really stupid financial mistakes in my life, God has always met all of my needs; He has in fact always given me and my family a "blessing so great (we don't) have enough room to take it in!" I'm not suggesting you can simply go out and continue to make bone-headed financial decisions and not pay a price for it. I've made them and paid a price, but God has been faithful to meet all of my needs in spite of them and blessed me beyond anything I deserve.

I have to confess I don't believe anyone has made dumber financial decisions than I have; I know you may find it hard to believe. But let me tell you, when I was young and newly married I borrowed money on a credit card (I knew better) to invest in Pesos. That's right, Pesos! The idea was the company I was investing in was doing a rate exchange to make money. They would buy the Pesos and wait for the dollar to go up in value against the Peso and exchange them for dollars to make income. Seriously, who even thinks that way besides me and the friend who talked me into it? I was receiving computer print outs that showed I was making great money on the exchanges almost daily. It was going so well I was thinking I might borrow more money to invest when the FBI found the man who created the scam in Las Vegas gambling all of my money away.

Here's the thing: God never said He would bless us and provide for all our needs as long as we only made wise financial decisions. (There are benefits to making wise financial decisions and God gives us a lot of direction about it. We will talk about this more in chapter 9.) He said He would bless us and provide for all of our needs when we put Him first in our finances. Throughout the horrible time of having to pay back a large credit card bill I could not afford from a stupid Peso investment, as a young husband and father I was still faithful to put God first through tithing. And He proved Himself true. I can't even work out on paper how we miraculously made it through that mess.

"Your crops will be abundant,
for I will guard them from insects and disease."

As you read this you are surely making the argument that you don't have crops. Let me put this verse into context with the whole passage; it is written to a culture that relied primarily on agriculture for their income. The greatest risk farmers faced would be insects and disease destroying their crops. God's promise here is: He will protect your business, your source of income, when you put Him first in your finances

> **God will not allow the enemy to destroy the work He has for you.**

through tithe. This is truly His economy. He is not saying you have job security right where you are for the rest of your life.

He is saying He will not allow the enemy to destroy the work He has for you to do according to His will.

> *"Your grapes will not fall from the vine*
> *before they are ripe…"*

I don't have any grapevines at my house either. In a vineyard one of the worst things that could happen would be for the grapes to fall off the vine before ripening and not be harvested properly. Unripe fruit fallen from the vine abdicates wine making, the purpose of growing grapes has become futile. God's promise here is that all we do to earn our income and the income itself will not be in vain, but rather used for His purpose in us and others in His perfect timing.

With the understanding that the agricultural reference translates into our lives as our income, our work, you can see the importance and power of how Proverbs 3:9-10 applies to your life: "*Honor the Lord with your wealth, with the first fruits of all your crops; then your barns will be filled to overflowing…*" (NIV). We honor God with our wealth first and foremost, as we talked about already, with the foundational base of giving the first 10% in tithe. The reference in these verses to "first fruits" points toward 10% giving. It's important to understand the clarity this term "first fruits" brings to the process of how to honor God with our wealth.

If you were given 10 one dollar bills how would you know which dollar bill of the 10 is the first fruit? Simple, it's the first one to be paid out. How tragic that the "first fruits" often goes to something or someone you would never claim as a priority over God, though it seemed right and necessary at the time, only to discover after paying for all of the other needs as "first fruits" God got the leftovers. But notice your business, your source of income, your provision is filled to overflowing when you put God first. "*...then your barns will be filled to overflowing...*" That is why it is so important to take a leap of faith, regardless of where you are at this very moment in your finances, and get started now.

STARTING WHEN THINGS ARE AT THEIR WORST

In 1 Kings 17:8-16 the concept of starting to trust God by giving to Him first is put to the ultimate test when things are at their worst for a widow living in Zarephath. God instructed the prophet Elijah to go to Zarephath where a widow would give him food. When Elijah encounters the widow for the first time she is gathering sticks to make a fire to cook the last meal for herself and her son. In the upcoming days she expected to starve to death since there was no more food. She had been reduced to a handful of flour and a little cooking oil. Elijah made her a promise that if she would do as he says: "*make a little bread for me first. Then use what's left to prepare a meal for yourself and your son,*" not only would she and her son be saved, but "*there will always be flour and olive oil left in your containers until the time when the Lord sends rain and the crops grow again!*" (1 Kings 17:14b).

Imagine the incredible amount of faith it must have taken for this widow to give a stranger the first part of the little she had left. For most, especially knowing she needed to feed her son as well as herself, this would have been asking too much. However, it's important we understand in the context of the

Old Testament; the prophet represented God to the people. Knowing this however, she did as the prophet instructed her. The results? "...*She and Elijah and her son continued to eat for many days. There was always enough flour and olive oil left in the containers, just as the Lord had promised through Elijah*" (1 Kings 17:15-16). Unlike the Old Testament, we live in the blessing of being able to approach God the Father personally as His children through Jesus.

> *We live in the blessing of being able to approach God personally.*

WHERE DO I GIVE?

Since the prophetic gifting in the New Testament is different than the Old Testament, the prophet is no longer the one who represents God to us; I no longer have Elijah to give to directly. Now where should I give? Be careful of anyone who says you need to give to them personally because they are the man or woman of God; and if you give to them God will bless you like He did the widow. I recently heard a teacher I have admired for several years say something to that effect and he concluded his talk by telling the people if they would come forward and lay their money at his feet then God would bless them like he did the widow. I was stunned and brokenhearted to hear those words coming from his mouth. Not only does no man or woman have the right to claim as such, but it comes across as arrogant and cocky. I simply prayed for him, knowing God does not tolerate such a thing. It was amazing to me, because within a matter of a few weeks after I heard that sermon he was no longer in the ministry.

THE QUESTION REMAINS: WHERE DO I GIVE?

God is specific when He gives us His financial plan to put Him first. *"Bring all the tithes into the storehouse so there will be enough food in my Temple"* (Malachi 3:10a). His expectation is you give back to Him at the place where you worship. It is so logical. You would not go to dinner at one restaurant and then pay for your meal at another. In the Old Testament it was the Temple. In the New Testament the tithe was given to the synagogue or church. Throughout the New Testament the community, or gathering of the Church, is called the Body of Christ; together we are His family. *"We are many parts of one body, and we all belong to each other"* (Romans 12:5b). *"You are members of God's family. Together, we are his house, built on the foundation of the apostles and the prophets. And the cornerstone is Christ Jesus himself. We are carefully joined together in him, becoming a holy temple for the Lord"* (Ephesians 2:19c-21).

Jesus' perspective of the Church is that we are His bride; He loves the Church and He died for the Church. Therefore, we must guard our thoughts and perspective of the Church. I think about how much I love my wife Kathy, my bride. You may disagree with me about anything, but the moment you start picking on my bride we would have a serious problem. And I know that my human love for Kathy is limited compared to Jesus' divine love for His Church.

Throughout my years in ministry some have told me the reason they don't give their tithe to their Church is they don't trust them to do the right things with God's money. In other words, they don't trust the leadership. There could be many reasons for this, it could even be a simple communication problem. However, my response to someone who feels this

> *You should be able to have confidence in your church leaders.*

way is to challenge them to prayerfully consider whether or not they are attending the right Church. You should be able to have complete confidence in your church leaders to use the tithe and offerings in the way God would lead them to live out the mission and vision for the Church in your community and beyond.

A NOTE FOR PASTORS AND CHURCH LEADERS

If you are a pastor or a church leader it is important you are using best practices when it comes to the fiduciary responsibility you have as a leader in the Church. While this is not a book for pastors and church government, I will share with you some of the best practices we have implemented at Alive Church to give our people absolute confidence. First, as a Pastor I am never the one who handles, or is responsible for, the tithe and offering. We have a fiduciary board, directed by specific guidelines in our bylaws, that does so. They have a clear-cut process in place for how the tithe and offering is counted and deposited. They alone approve the budget in cooperation with myself as the visionary.

Second, yes we have a budget. We make it available for anyone to see should they wish. The budget has built in guidelines to keep a balance of accountability and empower our leadership, including myself as the pastor, to do the work and ministry God is leading us to do as we live out our mission. Third, we do an annual audit at the end of each budget year; this is published, including problems and recommendations, and made available to all who are interested. The annual audit not only looks at the dollar amounts, but whether or not the agreed processes for handling money was adhered to as well. Fourth, each month our board of trustees does an audit of a budgeted area of their choosing to accompany the treasures report for that month.

THE MIRACLES FOR DIRK AND SAMANTHA

When I left the story of Dirk and Samantha at the beginning of this chapter, I told you they made the decision to put God first in their finances through tithe and God began to work miracles in their lives. The miracles included a job for Samantha, immediately increasing their income to cover all of the normal budgeted amount previous to tithing. The biggest hurdle they faced, as far as they were concerned, was navigating through the bankruptcy. (A quick word about bankruptcy, our laws allow it for those who get in trouble. It is not meant as a loop hole for one's advantage; Dirk and Samantha were not a couple taking advantage.) They were especially concerned how they'd explain to the bankruptcy judge they were giving 10% of their income to God first and still needed help from him to pay their bills. They were honest and candid and the judge was very favorable with them. Within months their lives had radically changed in every way imaginable financially. As you can imagine they are incredible advocates for trusting God with your finances by putting Him first through tithe.

Even more important than the financial blessing was the amazing spiritual growth that had taken place in their lives throughout the process. Their faith and trust in God has seen exponential growth. While they are grateful for how the law of the land helped them, they still don't like to talk about the bankruptcy of their past. They will also tell you there is a lot of pain that comes with the process. Not only have they continued to live in their decision to put God first in their finances through tithing, they have also implemented the best practices for personal finances, given to us in the Bible, to assure it never happens again and that they will prosper and be prepared for the future. We are going to unpack those practices in the next chapter.

CHAPTER 8

MANAGING THE FATHER'S BUSINESS

I love the outdoors; I love being in the woods and the wilderness. Because of this I have always had an affinity for Jeeps. I love the history, look and vision behind the Jeep. Choices and priorities meant I didn't own my first Jeep until our oldest children were college age and my youngest were just dipping into their teens. I had a great Jeep! I enjoyed my Jeep until I found myself in a financial position where owing on the Jeep would take away from the needs of our family. I knew I could sell it and have money left over, but I didn't want to at first. I came to the place where I felt very clearly the Lord speaking to me through prayer: "Do you drive the Jeep or is the Jeep driving you?"

There is nothing wrong with driving a nice vehicle, even your dream vehicle. God is not against nice transportation; what He is against is that we, as His children, would allow ourselves to be driven by a desire that would entrap us in any way. In chapter 3 we talked about how money is amoral, it's a necessity here on earth. It's the love of money that becomes a problem. *"For the love of money is at the root of all kinds of evil. And some people, craving money, have wandered from the faith and pierced themselves with many sorrows"* (1 Timothy 6:10). While I dare not make the same blanket statement about material possessions, the argument could be made that some things are of an immoral nature. However, it is also true most of our possessions are amoral. Having possessions is not typically the problem, it's whether or not our possessions have us.

I knew God wanted to do something in my life through the Jeep situation, and it truly had to do with teaching me about being a better manager of His possessions. Remember all the fries are His. He gave me the fries; He can take away the fries if He wants to, or He could bury me in fries. He is working on our relationship, and the goal is for my heart and life to be aligned with Him. It's not that He doesn't want me to have and enjoy something, unless it is something immoral; He wants nothing to come between me and Him. And there's more: He wants me to be financially fit to be in a position of doing what He would have me do or give. The Psalmist wrote this in Psalm 1:3 regarding those who make a choice to follow God and His ways: *"They are like trees planted along the riverbank, bearing fruit each season. Their leaves never wither, and they prosper in all they do."* He wants me to prosper.

> The goal is for heart and life to be aligned with Him.

DANGER, DANGER, DANGER!

Even as I write the words of the Psalmist I can hear a few gasps; some of you are wondering if I am teaching what has been termed "the prosperity gospel." No, the premise between the truth of what the Psalmist has written differs from the ideas that drive the prosperity gospel. The word prosper in this Psalm means to push forward toward all God created you to be in Him and for Him. Don't mistake the powerful truth of Philippians 4:19, as many will, to support getting all you desire versus God meeting all of your needs. "*And this same God who takes care of me will supply all your needs from his glorious riches, which have been given to us in Christ Jesus.*"

The prosperity gospel says God will give you whatever you want whenever you want for any reason you want. You will not find any promise of this in the Bible. Many have sought to take John 15:7 out of context believing He promises prosperity in answer to our prayers: "*But if you remain in me and my words remain in you, you may ask for anything you want, and it will be granted!*" Just this verse alone, taken out of context, sounds like I should be able to ask for the most expensive Jeep I want with everything on it and He will give it to me. And the narcissist in me likes that interpretation. But Scripture must be taken in context.

Jesus' meaning in John 15 is applicable to us as His followers; we are to bear the fruit He desires in our lives. So we can ask anything in connection to His will, purpose, and plan and expect Him to produce fruit in our lives as an answer. He is not saying every narcissistic craving we have will be granted if we ask Him for it. Can you imagine any

> *We can ask anything in connection to His will, purpose, and plan and expect Him to produce fruit in our lives.*

parent giving their children everything they ask for, good or bad? Actually we have seen this in our society and have also seen the devastating results of such actions.

Throughout all of the counsel of the Bible the fruit we see is the fruit of leading others to Jesus, and the fruit of the Spirit being lived out in our lives. I could make the argument I would be a much better pastor and lead more people to Jesus if He would just give me my Jeep! Even as we read these words it sounds stupid Why? Because that thinking is self-centered, it has nothing to do with what Jesus was talking about regarding our prayers being answered. His primary purpose is for us to stay in a healthy relationship with God the Father, free, forgiven and empowered to live out His purpose and plans.

YOU GET TO CHOOSE: PROSPERITY OR POVERTY

The Proverbs writer says, *"Good planning and hard work lead to prosperity, but hasty shortcuts lead to poverty"* (Proverbs 21:5). Let me ask you which one of those would you choose, prosperity or poverty? For many this creates a tension. So let me spell it out a little clearer. Throughout the Bible prosperity means to make progress, to have forward motion, to flourish or thrive regardless of conditions. Poverty is to be lacking, in need or want, to have none of the necessities of life. It's a no brainer.

We choose by how we prayerfully plan and work at managing His affairs. We are His managers. All the fries are His and He gives them to us for enjoyment. His expectation is we will be good, faithful managers of His stuff. As His followers, while managing our time, treasures and talents, we manage His business. To be trite with any of those three, time, talent and treasure, is to be an unfaithful manager of all He has entrusted to us. In my book, *Life Palette*, I talk a lot about how we should manage our time and talents in order to live life as the masterpiece God created us to be. This book is primarily about managing His treasure His way so we can live His masterpiece design.

Jesus used this illustration in Luke 16 to teach how His followers should handle worldly wealth: "*There was a certain rich man who had a manager handling his affairs. One day a report came that the manager was wasting his employer's money*" (Luke 16:1). The word manager describes someone who oversees or is in charge of the affairs or household of another. This person has the trust and confidence of the one who owns something. In this case the manager is "*wasting his employer's money.*" And we have this option when it comes to all God has given us: to waste His resources according to our own desires and will. Be sure to note the employer was not pleased: "*So the employer called him in and said, 'What's this I hear about you? Get your report in order, because you are going to be fired'*" (Luke 16:2).

This is a normal reaction from any employer towards an employee. For that matter, any owner of anything. When I had my Jeep I had friends who would ask to borrow it for a day to go four-wheeling in the mountains. I always loved sharing it with them. On different occasions I would have a friend say he would treat it like his own. I responded by saying, "No, I want you to treat it like it's mine." It is easy to slip into the mentality of treating the blessings of God as if we own them. He is saying we need to treat it all like it's His. He is the owner; He is the employer in this parable Jesus is teaching.

You would probably never blatantly set out to be a wasteful manager of all God has given you. Not only is it not spiritual, it doesn't even seem ethical from a worldly perspective. Yet, you can be wasteful in more subtle ways. First, you know you've got a problem if you consistently find yourself saying, "Money goes out as fast as it comes in, and I have no idea where it all goes." If you are unable to track how you are spending money, how will you know whether or not you are being faithful to do what God wants you to do with the money? The second more subtle way to be a wasteful manager is to not plan for the future. The writer said in Proverbs 21:5, "*Good planning*" is one of the key elements that leads to prospering.

> *Good planning is one of the key elements that leads to prospering.*

Third, being lazy is mismanagement: "*Good planning and hard work*" according to Proverbs go hand in hand. The fourth subtle way we can mismanage God's blessings is through foolish spending. Marketers have mastered the art of convincing us of what we need, therefore we often spend without first going to God in prayer; we quickly forget who is the Lord of the fries.

FAITHFUL WITH HIS BUSINESS

My prayer is, rather than allowing yourself to be wasteful with all God has blessed you with, you would intentionally choose to be faithful. Like any relationship, faithfulness builds trust in your relationship with the Father. As you are faithful with all He has entrusted to you, meaning to be faithful according to His plans and purposes, eventually He will trust you with greater things. In Luke 16:10-11 Jesus says, "*If you are faithful in little things, you will be faithful in large ones...And if you are untrustworthy about worldly wealth, who will trust you with the true riches of heaven?*" The money He empowers you to earn and how you choose to use it are clearly a spiritual issue according to Jesus' words.

The primary asset God's given you to manage is your life. When you are intentional about managing this gift and all He has entrusted to you as He directs, then He will trust you with more, "*the true riches of heaven.*" Parents understand this concept intuitively, though they may not transfer it to their relationship with God the Father. Chapter 3 illustrated this when talking about a child asking a parent for a pet. The parent allowed the child to start with a goldfish to show responsibility. My wife Kathy

> *The primary asset God's given you to manage is your life.*

and I chose to allow our kids to first get a goldfish before getting a golden retriever since daily responsibility is much less and the consequences less severe as they learned to care for it. Once they proved themselves responsible for a fish they were then trusted with a dog.

Jesus' words teach us this principle to a much greater degree when it comes to our spiritual journey and our relationship with Him. Worldly wealth is something that will pass away and is not something we can take with us; and we cannot guarantee our beneficiaries will not squander it. Therefore, He compels us as managers of all He has blessed us with to trust Him by managing as directed in His Word, knowing He trusts us with more when we have proven ourselves able to manage well the smaller amounts He has given us.

THE FREEDOM OF BEING A MANAGER RATHER THAN AN OWNER

There are amazing benefits to being a manager rather than an owner. As a manager of God's money and God's stuff I don't have to sweat it when there is a problem. I get to live in the freedom of knowing when there is a flat tire on my truck, I don't have a flat tire; instead I prayerfully talk to God about what He wants me to do about His flat tire. As the owner He is the authority and it is His responsibility to provide for a new tire or not; my responsibility is simply to be accountable to do what He gives me to do. When finances don't come in for the mission and vision we feel He has given us as a church, we don't have a financial need, God does. It's His church. We are only accountable to do what He wants with what He gives us. As the owner, should He choose to close the doors He can. And if He closes the doors it would be our job follow His lead.

> *You are only accountable to do what God wants with what God gives.*

Let me illustrate the freedom of being a manger rather than an owner with horses. I enjoy riding, but not trail riding with a guide who won't let you run the horses and worries about a person's level of experience. I like to ride occasionally but don't have a horse. I don't want a horse. A horse owner has to be available to feed and care for the horse twice a day at specific times, or have the means to pay someone to do it. I want neither. However, I have a friend who has horses and loves to care for them. It's his passion. He does it well. He also loves to have me join him for rides when I can. You can see the incredible benefit for me. Why would I want to be an owner when I benefit without the daily responsibility? How much more are we able to enjoy the benefits of all God provides in our lives knowing the responsibility is not on us alone?

THE REST OF MY JEEP STORY

I started this chapter by telling you about my Jeep and how God challenged me at one point with this question: "Do you drive the Jeep or is the Jeep driving you?" The rest of the story was an amazing journey for me in learning how to be a better manager of all His business. I sold the Jeep immediately and God was faithful to provide another car to drive with no debt. I knew that once I did what He wanted me to do with His Jeep, He had a problem to solve; His kid, me, didn't have a car to drive back and forth to work. So God had a transportation problem. As a manager of all that is His, I began communicating with Him about it through prayer. I wasn't begging for a new car or whining about a need but asking Him to reveal His plan.

A couple of days later one of my key volunteer leaders was walking down the hallway by the church offices, as he passed me he said, "Jeff I heard you sold your Jeep and are looking for something to drive around town. I got a beat up old Honda you can have." What an incredible blessing! I was so grateful. But you have to know for a Jeep guy, going from a really cool, manly Jeep to a Honda Civic was a little painful. Yet I knew God was working on me and my character.

Within a few days I went to the drive-through of our local pharmacy in my little Honda. I was used to sitting up high in my Jeep; everyone could see me. The Honda was so short I drove up without setting the buzzer off to alert the pharmacist of my arrival. After waiting, I finally had to pull out of the drive-through and go inside to get the prescription filled. I remember as I left the pharmacy praying, "OK God, I'm so grateful for this car You've given me to drive; it's Your car. And I don't want anything other than You and what You have for me, but couldn't I drive something more fitting of my personality?" Within a couple weeks another man from church called me: "Jeff, I'm retiring and I'm done with my work truck; it has a lot of miles on it, but I feel like I'm supposed to give it to you." (He had no idea I sold my Jeep and the whole Honda ordeal.) There were a lot of miles, 265,000, but it's a really cool looking, four-wheel-drive truck. And it fits me and my personality.

As I write this book, I am still driving that old truck. Now my son wants it. God's taking me somewhere on this journey; I'm trusting it's all His and I know I don't have to drive a Jeep. It's not that God doesn't want me to drive Jeep, eventually I hope to, it's just God doesn't want a Jeep to drive me. He doesn't want me as a manger of His stuff to put it before my relationship with Him as my loving Heavenly Father. He wants me, as one of His children, to enjoy His stuff; He does not want me to make my life about the stuff. As His son, I'm just a manager of His stuff and this is a place of absolute freedom!

Part of what He was doing was challenging me to live faithfully and completely as a manager. The more I do what He wants with His resources, as a manager, the more prepared I am to weather any potential financial storms that may come. After all, I can't tell you when or where these storms may pop up, I just know they are going to happen. I trust He knows and He is leading in such a way as to provide for all my needs regardless of future circumstances. This is what He wants for you too as His child. Read on to understand better how to weather financial storms and trust He is in control.

CHAPTER 9

WEATHERING FINANCIAL STORMS

In 1998 my friend Tony and I took our first exploratory trip to the Bay Islands of Honduras with plans for our church to do mission work. We traveled to the islands on the heels of Hurricane Mitch and saw destruction everywhere. From our boat on the ocean, as we traveled from one island to another, we could see the trees stripped bare of their branches as a result of 180 miles per hour sustained winds. Homes were destroyed. Bodies still lined the coastline because officials were overwhelmed trying to attend to all the needs. It was, to say the least, devastating. Similarly I traveled with another friend, Tom, in 2005 immediately after Hurricane Katrina brought its wrath to the Gulf Coast. The results were eerily similar to those Tony and I saw in the Bay Islands; the need for ministry and rebuilding was great.

In both instances our church partnered with local groups in those locations to help with the cleanup and rebuilding. The atrocious amount of destruction created by each storm was horrible for the people of those communities. I asked myself, "How do we prepare for disaster on that scale?" To be honest, there are some storms scientists, architects and engineers tell us regardless of how prepared we are we cannot survive. Such is the unbelievable force of nature.

Perhaps you or someone you know has gone through financial storms that were absolutely devastating. A medical crisis could financially ruin even the most prepared. Thankfully, storms like Mitch and Katrina are not the everyday norm of life. When they come, we must all gather around one another and rebuild. However, we need to prepare financially for the common storms of life. To assume storms are coming may seem a hopeless point of view at first. At Alive Church we always say: "You are either in a storm, just getting out of a storm or heading toward a storm." I understand this is not good news, but this is life. And even more importantly, once the storm hits it's too late to get prepared.

The good news is regardless of the storms we face – financial, physical, mental, spiritual or relational – God promises to be with us through the storms. He promises to go before us in the storm. He promises to meet our needs before

> **God promises to be with us through the storms.**

and during the storm. He promises to never leave us as we navigate the storm. And He promises to give us the strength and courage needed to persevere. "*When you go through deep waters, I will be with you. When you go through rivers of difficulty, you will not drown. When you walk through the fire of oppression, you will not be burned up; the flames will not consume you*" (Isaiah 43:2). Though we can and should depend on Him and His promises, we should also walk in wisdom and do our part to prepare in the ways He tells us to for the future. In talking about financial storms, as in all of life, there are seasons. "*He who gathers crops in summer is a wise son, but he who sleeps during harvest is a disgraceful son*" (Proverbs 10:5 NIV). In this book we especially want to look at how we should prepare in the season of prosperity for potential times of lack or worse – financial storms.

STORM PREPARATIONS

• Work

Work is a good thing. God gives us both provision and purpose in our work. As devoted followers of Jesus we work for Him: "*Work willingly at whatever you do, as though you were working for the Lord rather than for people*" (Colossians 3:23). Understanding we are working for the Lord in whatever we put our hands to, diligence rather than laziness is vital. Paul goes so far as to say, "*Those unwilling to work will not get to eat*" (2 Thessalonians 3:10b). There is great grace, and should be, for those who are unable to work. But those of us who are able to work, it's God's plan we work with great joy while serving and helping the disabled; He doesn't favor laziness. In 2 Thessalonians 3:12 Paul gives a command for people who are unwilling to work: "*We command such people and urge them in the name of the Lord Jesus Christ to settle down and work to earn their own living.*"

How we earn our living is also important; we are to have ethical standards that glorify God. Temptation abounds when it comes to unethical shortcuts, earning your living or

> *We are to have ethical standards that glorify God.*

building your business. My Grandmother used to say "A shortcut is the longest distance between two places." In other words, it will never end well; God will not be mocked. Working "as though you were working for the Lord rather than for people" means earning money His way – with integrity.

- Give to God first and yourself second

So far we discussed at great length God's system for trusting Him with our finances by putting Him first with tithe. This decision alone is the most important storm preparation any of us can do with what we have earned. The second most important storm preparation is to pay yourself. In other words save: "*The wise man saves for the future...*" (Proverbs 21:20a TLB). The last half of the verse is translated in the New Internal Version to say: "*...a foolish man devours all he has*" (Proverbs 21:20b). These words did not come from me; these words were penned by the writer of Proverbs; the Scripture tells us he was the wisest man to ever live apart from Jesus. Wise or foolish, the choice is ours based on whether we save or devour our income. Why? The purpose of saving for the future is preparation for both known and unknown future needs. Money is a tool to serve us. Beware of living this in reverse – serving money. And if we serve money rather than God we will spend our lives in futility trying to manage God. Let God be God, serve Him and manage His resources as directed.

Wisdom dictates we save for the future, not to be tight-fisted, stingy or driven by fear to count every penny, nickel and dime. Rather we plan for emergencies, unforeseen storms and things we know will eventually need to be replaced or repaired, while diligently saving what we can. And lastly we set aside money for future plans God is leading us toward. While God clearly tells us to be wise and save, do not forget money will never be able to save us. Be wise and live prepared for the storms by giving first to God and ourselves second.

- Stay well informed

I can't begin to tell you how often I have conversations with people in my office who are in a financial storm and have no clue of how bad the storm is at the moment. The tendency for many is to simply hope money struggles and problems will somehow resolve themselves magically if ignored long enough. This is not God's plan; His plan

> *Manage the money God has given according to His purposes and plans.*

is for us to manage the money He has given us according to His purposes and plans. Money has to be managed, it will not manage itself.

God requires we stay well informed of our business. And yes, each of us does have a business – the business of managing all He's given us for His glory. In Proverbs 27:23-24 God gives us a firm instruction regarding our business of living: *"Know the state of your flocks, and put your heart into caring for your herds, for riches don't last forever, and the crown might not be passed to the next generation."* The Proverbs writer is addressing a culture whose flocks were their business, their source of income. To bring this truth into the day and culture in which we live is to say, "We must stay well informed of what we own, owe, spend, invest and give." We are given this warning, applicable to all of life, in Hosea 4:6, *"My people are destroyed from lack of knowledge"* (NIV). We can only manage resources that we are well informed of. Staying well informed of all we own, owe, spend, invest and give is an essential financial storm preparation.

- Project your spending needs

When you are serious about getting your financial house in order as God's faithful manager, you will need to prayerfully project your spending needs as storm preparation. When my wife Kathy and I were younger we were not at all good at projecting. In fact, for many years we would get close to Christmas and realize we had not prepared for it. Amazing, to think it came every year on December 25th and yet we weren't projecting it into our budget until the moment we needed to go shopping. Now to be honest with you, the way we were able to get great at projecting our spending needs was to have Kathy take over the home finances; apparently it is not my gift. However, I am gifted at empowering those who are experts in areas I am not. This may be your talent as well. God has gifted us all differently; we need one another this way. Let me remind you of Proverbs 21:5 here: *"Good planning and hard work lead to prosperity, but hasty shortcuts lead to poverty."*

> *Planning for necessary spending is critical storm preparation.*

Planning for necessary spending is critical storm preparation because your financial stability and freedom is not a result of how much you earn, it is completely based on what you spend. To spend without thinking and planning is impulse spending. Marketers are depending on you to be impulsive. There is a big difference between saying "I can't afford it" and "I choose not to afford it" because I have prayerfully projected my spending needs and choose not to buy impulsively. When you allow others to tell you what you need and want, your money will disappear quickly.

This is not only important for those who don't make much, but perhaps more so for those who make a lot. The more money you the make the more entitled you may feel to buy whatever you want, whenever you want without prayerful consultation with the Father. It is surprising and amazing how many wealthy people end up in trouble during a financial storm because they did not project their spending. To truly be able to afford something, you must realize the projected cost of maintenance and insurance. Recently I watched a show about the lifestyle of the rich. They highlighted an astronomically expensive yacht. For those who could afford to pay for such a yacht, the salesman warned buyers to be prepared to spend $10,000,000 a year to keep it afloat. Your purchases may never be on the level of the extremely rich, but recognize everything you own comes with the expense of "keeping it afloat;" and alongside each projected expense you will need funds set aside in preparation for any storms that come your way.

- Be content

The last storm preparation is to learn contentment. *"Enjoy what you have rather than desiring what you don't have. Just dreaming about nice things is meaningless—like chasing the wind"* (Ecclesiastes 6:9). Discontentment will rob us of any enjoyment of the blessings God has already given us. We get overextended when we try to live the illusive dream marketers continually push, or when we attempt to live a lifestyle matching one of our neighbor's or friend's. We justify the decision to overextend, convincing ourselves it's a need not a greed. Yet God clears a path for us to enjoy His provision: "*Enjoy what you have...*" The Hebrews writer says, "*Don't love money; be satisfied with what you have*" (Hebrews 13:5a).

We were not created to find satisfaction in things, rather in relationship with God, our loving Heavenly Father, first and others second. In Him we can have contentment and truly enjoy all His blessings. "*Yet true godliness with contentment is itself great wealth. After all, we brought nothing with us when we came into the world, and we can't take anything with us when we leave it. So if we have enough food and clothing, let us be content*" (1 Timothy 6:6-8). Contentment is ours when we are thankful to God for all He has provided rather

> *Contentment is ours when we are thankful to God.*

than complaining about what we don't have; it's amazing how this attitude shift opens the way for greater joy in our lives.

You may have just read all of these storm preparations and said, "I don't like what God says and I want to handle my money my way." You are all free to choose to do things your way or God's. However, know this, when you choose not to do something God's way you are on your own. Good luck!

STORM WARNINGS

When your financial life is out of control, you can rest assured it is a symptom of something greater, an out of control life. We have looked at how to prepare for a potential financial storm. Now let's take a look at seven serious indicators you may be on the edge of a storm and what to do about them.

1. Maintaining your lifestyle through credit

For most of us it's fun to spend money; and our culture has made it easy to spend money we don't have. However, there are several problems with living on credit; the first and most important one is our loving Heavenly Father is working on our character as we grow in trust of Him as our provider: "*Yet true godliness with contentment is itself great wealth*" (1 Timothy 6:6). Second, as His followers we are not to live presumptuously about the future here

> **God promises to supply all of your needs.**

on earth: "*Don't brag about tomorrow, since you don't know what the day will bring*" (Proverbs 27:1). Spending tomorrow's money today reveals we are struggling with knowing the difference between needs and greeds. Remember God promises to "*supply all of your needs*" (Philippians 4:19) not our greeds; He loves us too much for indulgence.

2. Withholding payments or paying just the minimum

When you find yourself in a position financially of withholding payments from those you owe, you need to be aware a financial storm is brewing. In Romans 13:8a Paul writes, "*Let no debt remain outstanding, except the continuing debt to love one another..."* (NIV). Withholding, missing, perpetually making late payments or only making the minimum payment on a card balance are all indicators a storm is brewing if not already here.

3. Not able to live in God's financial system

Earlier we looked at God's system to put Him first in our finances through tithe. He is very serious about this: *"Should people cheat God? Yet you have cheated me! But you ask, 'What do you mean? When did we ever cheat you?' You have cheated me of the tithes and offerings due to me. You are under a curse, for your whole nation has been cheating me"* (Malachi 3:8-9).

My friend Ed once arrived to speak at a church in another country and was greeted at the airport by the hosting pastor and a friend. The friend offered to carry his luggage for him. Ed promptly asked, "Do you tithe?" The man responded honestly in front of his pastor and said, "No." Ed said, "I'll carry my own bags, if you will steal from God you will steal from me."

Very gutsy and kind of funny, but true. If you are a pastor or a church leader, you should be aware of whether or not the team you have serving with you is faithful to God's financial system or robbing Him. If they are willing to rob God of the tithe, why would you trust them with something so much more precious, His church?

If you are robbing God, you can't expect Him to bless you. This is a major red flag that there is a financial storm on the horizon.

4. Unable to pay Uncle Sam

Jesus was asked directly about the topic of whether or not we should pay our taxes to our government. His response was straight forward, "*'Here, show me the coin used for the tax.' When they handed him a Roman coin, he asked, 'Whose picture and title are stamped on it?' 'Caesar's,' they replied. 'Well, then,' he said, 'give to Caesar what belongs to Caesar, and give to God what belongs to God'*" (Matthew 22:19-21). I once accidentally shorted my tax payment by $.05, the first I knew of it was when I received a bill with penalties and interest of more than $2. I sent a check for $5 and never heard back. It just illustrates the importance of making sure we have our finances in order; imagine had that been a $100 or $1,000 mistake or more. I hear so many followers of Jesus speak against taxes, yet Jesus basically said just pay it. We have much more important Kingdom of God things to focus our energies on. If those of us living in the United States are not prepared to pay taxes on April 15th every year, a financial storm brewing.

5. Chasing get rich quick schemes

If you are always chasing get-rich-quick schemes you need to see it as a storm warning. I've already shared about my "peso investment" during my younger years; it was a get-rich-quick scheme no doubt. In spite of the embarrassment of such a poor decision I actually tried a couple of other quick money schemes. My uncle would call to share a new scheme he'd invested in with promises of this being the one to take care of us financially for the rest of our lives. Each of those schemes cost my family and myself money, putting us into debt. Not only that but it was an embarrassment as my eyes were opened to the fact I was actually scheming. By the time I was in my early thirties I realized this truth from the Bible: "*Good planning and hard work lead to prosperity, but hasty shortcuts lead to poverty*" (Proverbs 21:5).

We faithfully tithed during those embarrassing years and God faithfully met all our needs, but we were on a path to poverty. We made a decision we would never pursue another get-rich-quick scheme again. It took us years to get out of the debt we had incurred. But God, true to His Word turned the tide from a path of poverty to a path of prosperity. One of the most powerful lessons for me in making those poor decisions was how it affected every area of my life: the path of poverty relationally, mentally, and spiritually. I can't say this enough for any and all areas of our lives: there are no shortcuts! "*Good planning and hard work lead to prosperity...*"

6. Hiding from a spouse

A Gallup polled recently reported 64% of all couples fight over money; it is the number one cause for divorce in America. Of those who divorce, 54% cite the reason as money problems. Why? Money issues on your best days can be stressful; but if you are not trusting God and living within the system of His provision, they become overwhelming. The worst thing you can possibly do in any relationship is to hide money problems from your spouse. If you are in a relationship where you have no idea what's going on in the finances recognize this as a clear storm warning in your life right now.

> *The worst thing you can possibly do to hide money problems from your spouse.*

I can't tell you the number of times couples have sat in my office sharing that they are struggling in their marriage only to find out one of them is hiding financial problems from the other. You may not care about the finances and your spouse does, so you simply trust your spouse. This is not an issue of just trusting; it's an issue of walking in obedience to God together as a couple in the important area of finances. Both of you need to be well-informed of your finances, where you are headed and how well you are living out God's purpose and plan.

7. Extravagant spending versus extravagant giving

Extravagant spending is a storm warning, especially when compared to our giving. God, our loving Heavenly Father is an extravagant giver and His desire is for us to be like Him. If we are to live in the prosperous provision He has for us we must guard against extravagant

> *Extravagant spending is a storm warning.*

spending. "*Those who love pleasure become poor; those who love wine and luxury will never be rich*" (Proverbs 21:17). Extravagant spending is hard to define because it is different for each of us. It's personal. Recently, while watching TV, I saw a rich and famous person's log cabin valued at a mere $14 million dollars and it was just a vacation home. I thought I would love to be able to rent a log cabin for a few weeks in the mountains. Then, I realized that too could be extravagant in the eyes of some, based on current income. So, while extravagant living is a moving line for each of us, should it ever creep into our lives regardless of how much or how little we earn, it is a financial storm warning.

Extravagant giving on the other hand is much easier to define. It's not an amount or a percentage of income; it is a mindset and lifestyle as a follower of Jesus. In the next chapter we will unpack extravagant giving, what Jesus declares as the more blessed way to live.

CHAPTER 10

THE MORE BLESSED WAY

In Acts, Jesus' words speak of the blessing of living a generous life. He makes it clear it is the more blessed way to live. Acts 20:35b, *"You should remember the words of the Lord Jesus: 'It is more blessed to give than to receive.'"* His words, not mine. It seems counter-intuitive to the culture's daily, noisy pressure to believe, "The person with the most toys wins!" Do I truly believe Jesus' words? Is my desire to live as a giver greater than my desire to get more for me? I have to wrestle with whether or not I will live my life trusting Jesus' words will prove true in all I do. I will be more blessed by living a life of giving than I will by receiving.

The tension is real. Most of us wake up each morning and go to work with the expectation of earning at least the minimum amount to maintain our lifestyles. Don't believe it? What if our bosses or companies told us they would no longer pay us for our work? Immediately we all respond in a panic; we have bills to pay. I get it, I need to earn a living for myself and my family. Throughout the cycle of earning, providing for basic needs and paying bills we are held in a place of tension with relationship to Jesus' proclamation; the better way to live, the blessed way is to live a life of generosity.

Trusting Him as your provider completely and fully for all your needs yesterday, today and forever is the only path to peace amidst this daily tug of war between getting and giving. When you live in obedience and trust His call to give, you discover He already made provision, not only for what He would have you give but also for any void or need the choice to give may have created.

BLESSED TO BE A BLESSING

The nugget of truth buried within the words of Jesus is to live the more blessed way we must first receive. We see this in some of Jesus' most famous words: "*For God loved the world so much that he gave his one and only Son, so that everyone who believes in him will not perish but have eternal life*" (John 3:16). He gave. He made the first move so that we can receive. It is only in our receiving of Him, His eternal purpose and provision that we can understand the fullness of Jesus' truth: "*it is more blessed to give than to receive.*" And only in receiving His power are we capable of living the more blessed life as He did.

> *God blesses us so we can bless others.*

As we give our lives to Him, we receive the promise of His provision. He provides our time, talent and treasure. He blesses us in all of these so we can bless others: "*Yes, you will be enriched in every way so that you can always be generous*" (2 Corinthians 9:11a). We are blessed to be blessings. As we trust Him and He provides for our needs and more, He is wanting us to be faithful conduits.

104

When Kathy and I married, we served as worship leaders in a small town in West Texas. We just had our first child and money was tight. One Sunday morning after a church service, a man approached and told us he felt he was supposed to give us $100. He then handed us a $100 bill. We were very excited. Within a few hours we would be attending a ministry rally for the teenagers of our local high school. We quickly grabbed lunch and headed to the gym. There were no seats, so we stood along the wall of the high school gym as we listened to a visiting ministry team share Jesus' love with the teenagers of our community through a unique ministry. It was amazing and powerful; many teenagers responded that day and made decisions of faith. As the rally was coming to a close the leader of this ministry shared their financial needs and prepared to take an offering. But just before he prayed for the offering he hesitated, and as if it were an afterthought said, "I sense the Lord telling me there are 3 people here today who are to give $100 bills."

We had a choice to make in that moment. We could have determined, "No, we need this money." We could have struggled and wrestled with God reminding Him how much we needed the $100, and we could have easily justified it with Him. Instead, we knew immediately this was the reason God blessed us with the $100 bill; and we were excited to know God trusted us enough to be conduits. The man who had given us the money was not at the event. On our own we would have had no money to give. We recognized immediately we were blessed to be a blessing. We gave the $100 bill in the offering without hesitation. Since then God has used us in similar situations, and the more we live in faithfulness the more He will do so. Now, you need to know we are not perfect spiritual people who do it right every time. This was just an example of a time we were tuned in to what God was doing in and through us. Our desire is to be faithful in every moment of every day, however like you we struggle at times and continue to grow in this area of our lives. We have three attitudes to choose from when we face the struggle, with each blessing God gives us, between doing as He directs or deciding for ourselves.

ATTITUDES TOWARD GOD'S BLESSINGS

These three attitudes are not only found in the story of my interactions with my kids over french fries, but also found in one of Jesus' most famous parables, the parable of the Good Samaritan in Luke 10:25-37. A lawyer asked Jesus a question about eternal life; the man himself gives the answer when Jesus asks him what the law of Moses said regarding this: "'...You must love the Lord your God with all your heart, all your soul, all your strength, and all your mind.' And, 'Love your neighbor as yourself'" (Luke 10:27). Jesus affirms the answer: "Do this and you will live!" (Luke 10:28b). The counsel of all of Scripture is found here, applicable also to our finances, God first. But this man wanted to justify his actions toward others, so he pressed in with Jesus, "'And who is my neighbor?'" (Luke 10:29b).

To give clarity Jesus juxtaposed three different attitudes through the actions of thieves, an unloving Priest and a loving Samaritan. The Jews and Samaritans hated one another; the

Jews considered Samaritans to be completely non-religious people. Because the Jews knew themselves to be the true descendants of Abraham, they looked down on the Samaritans for intermarrying with other ethnicities; they were not children of Abraham. All of us live in one of the three attitudes when it comes to our money.

Sometimes we move from one to another depending on the day or situation. But Jesus obviously wants us to imitate Him and live in a specific attitude at all times as we see in the parable.

> *Jesus wants us to imitate Him and live in a specific attitude.*

ATTITUDE OF GREED

"*'A Jewish man was traveling on a trip from Jerusalem to Jericho, and he was attacked by bandits. They stripped him of his clothes, beat him up, and left him half dead beside the road'*" (Luke 10:30). These robbers didn't just steal the man's money or possessions; they stripped him of his clothing, beat him and left him for dead. In other words, the man was in desperate need of someone to help otherwise he would die. How many times have we seen a person or group of people left physically and emotionally destitute from the hurt and pain caused by someone's greed?

The greedy actions of the robbers came from an attitude of entitlement; I deserve what you have, even though I have not earned it, therefore I will take it regardless of who gets hurt along the way. Greed is the attitude found in the robbers. Perhaps as you read this you respond, "I'm not a robber. I would never steal from others what I have not earned." The attitude of greed reveals itself with much greater subtleties in our lives: discontent and coveting. Paul tells us in Romans 13:9, "*For the commandments say, 'You must not commit adultery. You must not murder. You must not steal. You must not covet.' These—and other such commandments—are summed up in this one commandment: 'Love your neighbor as yourself.'*"

The attitude of greed will reveal itself through hoarding or miserly behavior. The root word of miserly is miser, and miser is derived from miserable or wretched. This attitude steals the joy of living the "*more blessed way*" Jesus wants for us. Jesus said, "*Watch out! Be on your guard against all kinds of greed; a man's life does not consist in the abundance of his possessions*" (Luke 12:15 NIV). While we cannot take it with us to heaven

> *Miser is derived from miserable or wretched.*

we can send it on ahead by being faithful to invest in His Kingdom: "*Teach those who are rich in this world not to be proud and not to trust in their money, which is so unreliable. Their trust should be in God, who richly gives us all we need for our enjoyment. Tell them to use their money to do good. They should be rich in good works and generous to those in need, always being ready to share with others. By doing this they will be storing up their treasure as a good foundation for the future so that they may experience true life*" (1 Timothy 6:17-19).

The attitude of greed is destructive in your relationship with God and others. You cannot maintain a growing, healthy relationship with your loving Heavenly Father without expressing love to those around you. Greed is like an unattended cancer in the body, it will spread death and destruction over everything God intends for good in your life.

Greed will cause you to measure your self-worth by what you own or don't own, rather than by the One who loves and created you.

ATTITUDE OF SELFISHNESS

The second attitude Jesus reveals in response to the question, *"And who is my neighbor?"*, is selfishness. This attitude is found in those whom you would expect to show compassion: *"By chance a priest came along. But when he saw the man lying there, he crossed to the other side of the road and passed him by. A Temple assistant walked over and looked at him lying there, but he also passed by on the other side"* (Luke 10:31-32). Both the priest and the temple assistant aided in leading worship in the temple. At this time in history, because of their leadership and office, the Old Testament law demanded they provide care for the man left for dead. But they didn't.

It may be they were more concerned with following the rules and regulations required of priests and temple assistants in order to maintain their positions. The man may have appeared dead and to touch a dead body rendered them "unclean" and therefore unable to lead in the temple worship for a period of time. The decision to choose rules and regulations over relationships is what many find deplorable in those who call themselves religious. Regardless of their reasoning, those we would expect to reach out and help the most, refused.

Of the three attitudes found in this parable we all start with selfishness. Think about it for a moment, have you ever seen parents teaching their toddler to be selfish? No. Why? Because they don't have to, it's innate within us all. No one taught us to say, "mine" when another child wanted to play with our toys. Instead, most parents focus on teaching toddlers to share, to live generously. Yet the attitude of generosity often falls on deaf ears when we are children and it remains latent

> *All of us live in one of the three attitudes.*

until just the right moment when our selfishness is exposed in adulthood – the moment when we think, "I work hard for my stuff and its mine, it's not God's." (Those are my fries!) And yet God as your loving Heavenly Father gives you all things to leverage for His sake and for His Kingdom's sake on earth and for eternity, "*Don't be selfish; don't try to impress others. Be humble, thinking of others as better than yourselves. Don't look out only for your own interests, but take an interest in others, too*" (Philippians 2:3-4). Can we ever imagine Jesus having had a selfish attitude when He was called upon to go to the cross and pay the penalty for our sins?

ATTITUDE OF GENEROSITY

The third attitude in Jesus' parable of the Good Samaritan is generosity. "*Then a despised Samaritan came along, and when he saw the man, he felt compassion for him. Going over to him, the Samaritan soothed his wounds with olive oil and wine and bandaged them. Then he put the man on his own donkey and took him to an inn, where he took care of him. The next day he handed the innkeeper two silver coins, telling him, 'Take care of this man. If his bill runs higher than this, I'll pay you the next time I'm here'*" (Luke 10:33-35). This is the attitude we, who are followers of

Jesus, are called to live. This is the attitude Jesus said is the *"more blessed way"* to live.

While the robbers, the priest and the temple assistant were more concerned for themselves, this Samaritan, despised by Jesus' listeners, served the man who was left for dead. Jesus' clarity of how to love your neighbor involves the freedom to live generously, knowing, understanding and trusting that all you have is provided by God for God's purposes. This Samaritan man not only attended to the physical wounds but, at his own expense, cared for the man. The Samaritan excelled in generosity. He made sure the wounded man's immediate needs were met and said, "*'Take care of this man. If his bill runs higher than this, I'll pay you the next time I'm here.'*" How would your life, and our world, be different if followers of Jesus made it their goal to live as Paul tells us to in 2 Corinthians 8:7? "*Since you excel in so many ways—in your faith, your gifted speakers, your knowledge, your enthusiasm, and your love from us —I want you to excel also in this gracious act of giving.*" While we should focus on excelling in our faith, speaking, knowledge, enthusiasm and love, Paul tells us we should excel in giving as well – an attitude of generosity. The hesitancy for many is it feels too costly, yet Jesus leads the way in this attitude as our example. "*For God called you to do good, even if it means suffering, just as Christ suffered for you. He is your example, and you must follow in his steps*" (1 Peter 2:21).

The question is: "*And who is my neighbor?*" The answer Jesus taught is to be generous in showing love toward anyone in need, and it may be costly. Yet, Jesus tells us generosity is the more blessed way to live. "*You should remember the words of the*

Lord Jesus: 'It is more blessed to give than to receive'" (Acts 20:35b). Without first trusting God as our provider, Jesus' more blessed way of living seems overwhelming. Let's not miss the blessings God has for us by convincing ourselves we cannot live a life of generosity. We must resist the enemy's attempts to rob us of living a life of blessing.

TO LIVE IT THINK THIS WAY

To live the *"more blessed way"* there are three patterns of thought you must embrace. First, always think attitude over amount. Generosity is not about the amount, it's about the attitude – having and living the attitude of Jesus. Imagine if everyone came with an attitude of generosity into your home, your church, or your work. Think in terms of what you can do to be a blessing of generosity today.

> **Always think attitude over amount.**

Second, think stewardship over ownership. Stewardship means He owns it all and I am, by His power living in me, managing all He has entrusted to me. Stewardship declares all the fries are His to begin with and *"No one can receive anything unless God gives it from heaven"* (John 3:27b). I am just a conduit.

Third, always think about worship rather than worth. When the Lord Jesus leads you to give something you think is of great worth, or some challenging amount, don't let the value cause hesitation. It's more important you develop the habit of living a life of generosity as worship than to consider the worth of earthly things. While the principle of sowing and reaping is always active in a life of generosity, this way of living is an act of worship to get more of God, not more stuff.

> *The principle is an act of worship to get more of God, not more stuff.*

I have to tell you I love writing my tithe check, or at least I used to. We give our tithe through our churches online portal nowadays rather than checks. The reason I love it and look forward to it is I have discovered Jesus' words to be true; this is the more blessed way to live. Kathy and I recently had a business deal we had been working on. In the process of closing the deal, Kathy asked me when it would close so we could give the tithe. We both agreed we couldn't wait to give. Why? We understand the principle Jesus taught, "*it is more blessed to give than to receive.*" The Proverbs writer said it this way, "*The generous will prosper; those who refresh others will themselves be refreshed*" (Proverbs 11:25).

As we come to the end of this chapter, I understand many of you who are reading this may feel a sense of discouragement. While you may see the truth of Jesus and His Word throughout this book, you have simply allowed yourself to get in a position of overwhelming debt and see no hope of moving forward in this incredible journey God has for you. Kathy and I have been there. We understand. Read on. In the next chapter we are going to look at some practical everyday things you can do to get to a place where you can live in freedom and generosity.

CHAPTER 11

FREEDOM

When I write or read the word "freedom" my mind always goes to the last scene of the movie, Brave Heart. William Wallace, played by Mel Gibson, screams it at the top of his lungs, "FREEEEEDOOOM!!!" It moves me, mostly because freedom is one of the five personal core values I have chosen to live by since my early 20s. This value has shaped many of my life decisions including the choice to follow Jesus; I have found ultimate freedom in Him. It also shapes my passion to teach about God's principles for handling finances His way because when we do we experience financial freedom.

Our culture of instant gratification leads us to financial enslavement and ultimately robs us of freedom. The Proverbs writer tells us, "*the borrower is the servant to the lender*" (Proverbs 22:7b). Yet we are bombarded with the "buy now, pay later" mentality. We are told we deserve the things we want and shouldn't have to wait to have them. As we are being sold this bill of goods the one word all of the marketers avoid

> *Our culture of instant gratification leads us to financial enslavement.*

is debt, but that is what they are selling to us in the form of a loan.

When you are in debt you are a servant to the lender. Don't believe it? Call one of the companies you owe money and tell them you want to take a few months sabbatical from making the payments. You already know how that would go; because in reality when you owe someone money you are a servant of obligation. There is nothing about this truth to celebrate. In fact, I hate it because I am passionate about freedom, mine and yours. How does the idea of being enslaved with debt make you feel?

Many of you reading this know firsthand. I know; I've been there, done that and done it again. I got the tee-shirt. The feelings, the emotions, the weight of debt is the exact opposite of what God wants you to experience. He wants you to experience freedom. *"For the Lord is the Spirit, and wherever the Spirit of the Lord is, there is freedom"* (2 Corinthians 3:17). How foolish to think He wants you to be free from sin, yet to live in bondage in other areas of your life. God is a God of freedom. In John 8:36, Jesus said, *"So if the Son sets you free, you are truly free."* Lord of the Fries is about the incredible truth Paul gives us in Philippians 4:19, *"And this same God who takes care of me will supply all your needs from his glorious riches, which have been given to us in Christ Jesus."* It is incongruent to think for a moment He would provide for your needs by making you a slave to others through debt.

> *The weight of debt is the exact opposite of what God wants you to experience.*

YOU ARE CALLED TO FREEDOM

If you have made the decision to follow Jesus then you are called to live in freedom. *"For you have been called to live in freedom, my brothers and sisters. But don't use your freedom to satisfy your sinful nature. Instead, use your freedom to serve one another in love"* (Galatians 5:13). If you are still considering putting your faith in Jesus you need to see freedom as one of the many incredible benefits. Notice in Galatians 5:13 Paul said *"not to use your freedom to satisfy your sinful nature,"* the *very thing marketers are working to get you to do. Rather you are to "use [y]our freedom to serve one another in love."*

Let me illustrate this with a personal, real-life scenario. My second daughter Kadi serves as a missionary through YWAM (Youth With A Mission). When she was young I took her on a mission's trip to Honduras and she was hooked. She was very intentional about where she went to college, what she drove and how she lived so she could stay debt free. She learned in her youth the *"borrower is servant to the lender."* When the time came for her to go and serve in mission work she was completely debt free; she was a servant to no person or institution. When she felt the Lord prompting her to "go" she was free to go and serve, and her obedience to the call has taken her around the world four times.

> **When you owe someone money you are a servant.**

I can't tell you how many times I have shared her story and the ways the Lord uses her to serve others around the world only to hear this statement, "I wish I could do that." I always say, "You can. Go do it if that is what the Lord is leading you to do." The number one response is, "I can't, I have too much debt." How sad to think anyone would not be able to answer the call, take advantage of the opportunities or experience the purpose God has for them because they have allowed themselves to become a "servant to a lender."

Yet this is exactly how many people live. Perhaps as you read this you feel hopeless because of the insurmountable debt you have acquired. You may feel as if I am writing your story. There is something you know God wants you to do, something you are passionate about and would do if you could, but you feel trapped by debt. The freedom to obey Him has been surrendered to the lender you have borrowed from and are currently serving financially. I'm here to tell you, there is a way out! I'm here to tell you regardless of how trapped you feel right now, God's plan and purpose is for you to experience "FREEEEEDOOOM!!!" If you will follow God's financial plan and the steps lined out in this chapter for getting out of debt, you can live in freedom. I can give you many, many examples of those I have seen over the years who have done so.

BUT IT'S NOT GOING TO BE EASY

I hope the previous paragraph gets you pumped up, salivating to live in the freedom God has for you in every area of your life and particularly in the area of finances. But I must tell you at this point, it's not going to be easy. If you are living a lifestyle predisposed to debt, you need to

A follower of Christ lives with integrity.

know getting into debt is much easier than getting out of debt. It's going to take discipline, courage, endurance, persistence, character and integrity; all of which Jesus gives you as you depend on Him and obey Him. You will not accidentally quit being a servant to your lenders, it will require intentionality. No one just coasts out of debt, this is an uphill climb. But it's worth it because on the other side of the summit is freedom. And you were made to live in freedom!

WHY WE GET INTO DEBT

There are as many specific reasons for getting into debt as there are individuals. However, most of them fall into a few overarching categories, all of which marketers focus on. First is discontentment. It is amazing how a slick ad on TV can take you from contentment with your car to incredible discontentment in a few seconds. It works, you weren't even considering getting a new car, but now you are shopping. After all, your old car just won't do and you deserve a better car – one that's safer and will give you greater joy. Lest you think there is something wrong with having and driving a nice new car, that is not what I am saying. This is about whether or not you can or should afford the nice new car. Will you

> **Guard your contentment.**

have the car – the debt – or will it have you? Paul tells us in 1 Timothy 6:6, *"true godliness with contentment is itself great wealth."* Guard your contentment, don't let marketers stir up discontentment that can easily lead to debt.

The second reason we easily allow debt to mount in our lives is a lack of self-control. If you are a follower of Jesus you have self-control. *"But the Holy Spirit produces this kind of fruit in our lives: love, joy, peace, patience, kindness, goodness, faithfulness, gentleness, and self-control"* (Galatians 5:22-23a). The character of Christ in you is producing self-control. Regardless of your financial status, whether or not something is affordable, walking in self-control demands you always pray before we pay. It is dangerous to think just because I have enough money I can do whatever I wish. God will not bless your narcissism, He has a plan and a purpose with each blessing. The Spirit of self-control will not only help you stay out of debt but give clarity to all you are to do with all He has entrusted to you according to His purpose and plans.

Along with self-control there must be a willingness to sacrifice. You have been sold a bill of goods: you don't need to wait to have your desires fulfilled. Young couples are trying to live the lifestyle of their parents without making the sacrifices and investments parents made for such a lifestyle. Unfortunately, this kind of thinking will cost much more over the course of time and keep you in financial slavery to debt.

Third, debt mounts quickly because you are searching for significance in all the wrong places. The very thing God has created for you to find in Him – significance – you are influenced to find elsewhere. The desire itself is good. God wants you to live a life of significance simply by embracing the life He has created for you with Him living in you. The deception that you will find significance in anything besides Him allows you to willingly dive into financial slavery through debt.

Status is the fourth reason debt is so prevalent in our culture. This concept is often described as keeping up with the Joneses. Don't be fooled though, the Joneses are trying to keep up with the Joneses as well. *"Some who are poor pretend to be rich; others who are rich pretend to be poor"* (Proverbs 13:7). No one wants to live as a poser; yet our culture masquerades a lifestyle, overwhelmingly so, by financing it with debt.

The fifth and final reason we go into debt is a lack of planning. In Proverbs 21:5 the writer states, *"Good planning and hard work lead to prosperity, but hasty shortcuts lead to poverty."* Consider this verse for a moment. If given a choice would you choose prosperity or poverty? In chapter 8 we defined the biblical concept of prospering as a means to push forward toward all God created you to be in Him and for Him. Poverty is to live in need through lack of provision. Desiring to live the life He created you for requires you to be a good planner and a hard worker, both of which can be learned. A lack of either will often result in a lifestyle of debt.

WHAT TO DO ABOUT IT

Regardless of the reason, you or someone you love is living in the slavery of debt and the path forward is one of a new direction. *"Seek his will in all you do, and he will show you which path to take"* (Proverbs 3:6). It's time to take a new path, correct your course. The destination of a path will not change;

> *The destination of a path will not change; you must choose another path.*

you must choose another path. Let me illustrate. We were traveling with friends on a vacation to southern Missouri.

121

Their family was traveling in their car and their dad was not good with directions. We spent the night in Amarillo, Texas. The next morning after breakfast we headed out. I didn't see their car on the highway for several moments and decided to contact them making sure they were not having problems. He quickly assured me things were fine and they were not far behind. I slowed and waited, still nothing. I finally asked him to read the highway signs to me as he passed them. He was traveling on I-40 west and he was going the wrong direction.

What should he do? Should he keep going and hope they would get to Branson, Missouri via Los Angeles? No, that sounds ludicrous even as you read it. Simple, get off of the highway and head in the other direction. Why? Because a specific destination is not reached through sincerity or hope; destination is reached only by going the right direction. Debt is the wrong direction financially. Moving toward a life of freedom from debt begins with a change of direction – one leading to destination "debt free". So, let's get started.

Here are seven course corrections you need to make to begin this journey.

1. Make a declaration that you are going to live financially free.

Don't start tomorrow or next week or next month, make a declaration to begin right now as you read these words. From a biblical perspective this is important. *"The wicked borrow and never repay, but the godly are generous givers"* (Psalms 37:21). To continually live in debt and not repay is wicked. God doesn't just say it's a bad idea or it may cause a few problems here and there, He says it is wicked. As follower of Jesus, when you make a promise you are expected to keep it. Make a declaration now that you will not only repay all you owe but will begin living financially free from now on.

2. Take an inventory.

The second course correction is getting a clear picture of your current financial situation. You need to know how much you owe and all that you own. Perhaps up to this point you believed ignorance was bliss or you knew it wasn't, but you just couldn't face the music. It's time. Living in financial ignorance is a path to disaster, regardless of how much you make. You need to know how much you make and where it is going. Money doesn't just simply disappear; you are allowing it to go somewhere by your choices. It's time to make new choices. The interest clock is ticking so action is imperative.

> *It's time to make new choices.*

3. Develop a repayment plan.

Now that you truly know where you are financially, don't get depressed; prayerfully begin developing a repayment plan. Remember according to Proverbs 21:5, "*Good planning and hard work lead to prosperity, but hasty shortcuts lead to poverty.*" You may have stumbled into debt, but you will never stumble out; it's going to take good, intentional planning. Start making your plan by committing the need to God in prayer. Seek out a good, biblical-based, financial counselor so you will not be taken down a worldly path. "*Plans go wrong for lack of advice; many advisers bring success*" (Proverbs 15:22).

Make sure they are committed to helping you navigate toward living debt-free and honoring God with your finances.

Once you establish a repayment plan, sit down with your creditors and share the plan with them. I'll never forget the pain of doing this after Kathy and I sought financial counseling and developed a repayment plan. But it worked! After clearly communicating the plan to our creditors we found most of them agreeable to work with us as long as we remained committed to following our plan.

4. Simplify, simplify, simplify.

You've taken an inventory, so you know what you owe and what you own. You have a plan to move forward. Now look at how you can simplify your life and speed up the process of getting free from debt. What can you sell that you no longer need or use? When you sell it make sure you put all the money toward your debt. Don't overlook something simply because it's paid off. The cost of maintaining things through insurance and repairs can be a financial drain, especially for financed items. I once had a mentor tell me if you saw a man driving a fancy car with bald tires he really can't afford the car.

As you choose to let stuff go and put the money toward debt you will begin to relieve the tension caused by the debt. And you will have a sense of a "win" with every step you take toward full repayment of your debt. Prayerfully simplify. Consider everything; ask the Lord to show you what you should sell and make provision to sell it. When you sense God leading you to sell something and argue with Him about it, or simply refuse, beware. That item has become an idol in your life and you have put it before God.

In Matthew 19 Jesus was asked by a young man of great wealth what he would have to do to receive eternal life? Jesus told him, *"'If you want to be perfect, go and sell all your possessions and give the money to the poor, and you will have treasure in heaven. Then come, follow me.' But when the young man heard this, he went away very sad, for he had many possessions"* (Matthew 19:21-22). Jesus was not telling everyone to sell everything. The problem this young man had was his stuff had him; he was unwilling to put God first. As you simplify, prayerfully ask God what should go knowing you are choosing to put Him first above all things.

5. Pay off the smallest debt first.

When Kathy and I first started paying off debt the current thinking was to always pay off the debt with the highest interest rate first. We started down that road. A few months into the process Kathy figured out if we payed off the debt we owed the least amount on first, and then put all of that payment toward the next smallest debt we would get out of debt much faster, and we did. Since that time this has become common thinking,

> *Add the payment amount toward the next smallest debt.*

especially with great financial counselors like Dave Ramsey and his Financial Peace University. I'll never forgot when I first shared this idea with my church. My CPA was sitting in the audience. Afterward he challenged me that I should tell everyone to pay off the highest interest first. I asked him to go home and do the math. He did. The next week he told me he was going to encourage all of his clients to use the strategy of paying the smallest debt first. Warning: when you pay off a debt be sure to add the payment amount toward the next smallest debt. Don't go out and celebrate by getting into more debt.

6. Never give up.

I love the Winston Churchill quote: "Never, never, never give up." Paul writes in Galatians 6:9, "So let's not get tired of doing what is good. At just the right time we will reap a harvest of blessing if we don't give up." This will take time, effort, discipline and sacrifice. Imagine how different your life will be when you are living free from the slavery of debt. Imagine what you might do for God, or how you might live out the visions and passions He's given you in a different way. Never give up.

I promised seven but only listed six because the seventh course correction, in truth, should be the first. Making the final course correction gets God involved in the other six. This allows Him to work supernaturally in ways you cannot imagine. The next chapter is all about making course correction number seven so you can live in "FREEEEEDOOOM!!!"

CHAPTER 12

GOD'S GUARANTEE

I usually teach on this subject once a year at our church. I end the topic with God's guarantee for those who will take this last course correction toward living in God's financial plan. Again, it is truly the starting point as a follower of Jesus. Once you make the decision to cross the line in faith and trust God in this area of your life, your finances, your spiritual growth will abound. This is why I offer the guarantee. It goes something like this: "If after having been faithful to tithing for 90 days you don't feel God kept His promise, providing for all your needs, we will return all of the money you've given to our church during this 90 day challenge." You may wonder how I can be so confident as to offer a 90 day money back guarantee. The answer is simple, either God keeps all of His Word or we can't trust Him with any of His Word.

Remember: He promises, when we are faithful with our finances to trust Him in tithing, to open the storehouses of heaven and pour out a blessing so great we cannot contain it. *"'Bring all the tithes into the storehouse so there will be enough food in my Temple.' If you do,' says the Lord of Heaven's Armies, 'I will open the windows of heaven for you. I will pour out a blessing so great you won't have enough room to take it in! Try it! Put me to the test! Your crops will be abundant, for I will guard them from insects and disease. Your grapes will not fall from the vine before they are ripe,' says the Lord of Heaven's Armies. 'Then all nations will call you blessed, for your land will be such a delight,' says the Lord of Heaven's Armies"* (Malachi 3:10-12).

I'll never forget when I first became a pastor and decided to do this. I was so excited as I told the Elders in our church about my plan. While they all appreciated my enthusiasm and faith, one of them spoke up and said, "We should start setting aside a certain amount for those who are going to ask for their money back after the 90 day challenge is over." Chuckling, I challenged them to think about what was just said and to consider whether or not they believed God kept His Word. It took only a moment before we were all laughing as we recognized the inconsistency of this statement with what we all believed, through faith and personal experience; God would indeed do what He said He would do. We offered the challenge that first year and every year since.

> **The 90 day challenge.**

While I can't offer this guarantee to people who do not tithe to the church I pastor, I challenge everyone to put God to the test with their finances and let Him prove Himself faithful and true. You do your part and He will always do His as promised *"...open the windows of heaven for you. I will pour out a blessing so great you won't have enough room to take it in!"*

FOUR KEY ELEMENTS TO TITHING

There are four key elements you must understand about tithing as you put God to the test through this challenge:

First: the first 10% of your income belongs to God. The principle here is to put God first in your finances. Whatever you put God first in, He blesses. Throughout this book we have camped on this truth: it is God's plan for us to trust Him in our finances and as we do He will "...*supply all your needs from his glorious riches, which have been given to us in Christ Jesus*" (Philippians 4:19). Giving a percentage less than 10% is not tithing; the word for tithe actually means 10%.

God's financial system requires faith and trust – putting Him first and trusting Him to provide. Giving God the leftovers does not require faith; He does not want the leftovers. Obedience to His system is a reminder of Who He is, Lord of all, and His right to be given first place. This is a way to honor Him in your life: "*Honor the Lord with your wealth and with the best part of everything you produce. Then he will fill your barns with grain, and your vats will overflow with good wine*" (Proverbs 3:9-10).

The second key element of tithing reminds us giving more than 10% is not tithing. Here is the clear distinction between tithe and offerings. The tithe is the first 10% of my income and an offering is giving over and above the first 10%. Many people tell me they have decided to tithe more than 10%.

> *Giving more than 10% is not tithing.*

They are disappointed when I tell them it is impossible to do. Then I explain to them while you can give a greater percentage of your income to God everything above 10% is an offering. I'm all for increasing the percentage of giving once you've become faithful with the tithe and are ready to move into a lifestyle of generosity.

It is important to understand tithing is not giving; tithing is returning to God what is already His. Remember He owns all the fries, He can take all the fries and He can bury you in fries if He so chooses. In returning the first 10% of my income to Him through tithing I acknowledge I trust Him, not money, as my provider.

The third key element warns: to keep what belongs to God is stealing. We addressed this in Chapter 9 through Ed's luggage story. To use what God has set aside as the tithe for something else is stealing from Him. This may sound harsh but these are His words, "*Should people cheat God? Yet you have cheated me! But you ask, 'What do you mean? When did we ever cheat you?' You have cheated me of the tithes and offerings due to me. You are under a curse, for your whole nation has been cheating me*" (Malachi 3:8-9). When you put your faith in Him as your loving Heavenly Father, He has a right to whatever He asks of you. To continually trust Him with all things first and foremost is His financial system for you; and He has promised to those who trust in obedience to meet all of their needs. Notice should you choose to steal the tithe from God, you will not receive His blessing on your finances, your finances will be cursed.

Our final and fourth key element is to understand where the tithe is to be given. Notice in Malachi God says: "*Bring all the tithes into the storehouse so there will be enough food in my*

Temple" (Malachi 3:10). We addressed this in chapter 7 when we talked about eating in one restaurant and paying in a different one. It is important to recognize tithing not only as God's financial system for putting Him first in our lives, but as the method He uses for His Church, the Body of Christ, to live out the Great Commandment and Great Commission.

> *"Jesus replied, 'You must love the LORD your God*
> *with all your heart, all your soul, and all your mind.'*
> *This is the first and greatest commandment. A second*
> *is equally important: 'Love your neighbor as yourself.'*
> *The entire law and all the demands of the prophets are*
> *based on these two commandments."*
> Matthew 22:37-40

> *"Therefore, go and make disciples of all the nations,*
> *baptizing them in the name of the Father and the Son*
> *and the Holy Spirit. Teach these new disciples to obey*
> *all the commands I have given you."*
> Matthew 28:19-20a

My friend, Tom, started attending our Church during this teaching series. He promptly found me after the service and told me he loved me and he loved the church, but he and his wife gave their money to other missions and missionaries. They would occasionally give offerings to our church to help out, but he wanted to make sure it was OK for them to continue attending since they wouldn't tithe to our church. Of course I wanted him to attend regardless of his decision regarding his finances. However, I challenged him to go home, read Malachi 3, pray and consider what God would have him do. He found me first thing the following week before service to tell me he clearly understood what God said in His Word about the "storehouse." He and his wife prayed about it and would begin to tithe to our church. He asked for prayer because he believed the Lord wanted him to continue giving 10% of his income to the missions and missionaries he'd been supporting, and he recognized this was an offering above and beyond the tithe.

I was so excited for Tom. Not because I was the pastor of the church receiving his tithe. I know very well God doesn't need Tom's money, what He wants is what it represents, his heart. Tom's journey over the next year was unbelievable. Tom was faithful to tithe and do as the Lord had asked him: to give a 10% offering to other missions and missionaries. He reported the blessings God brought into his life that year. God had proven Himself faithful by opening "the windows of heaven" in response to Tom's obedience. That year Tom's business income quadrupled; he has not turned back from being faithful to tithe to God in his local church. Tom is a big advocate of God's financial system of tithing. He has shared his story in several of my weekend talks since the time he first heard me speak on the subject.

Tom's story is not your story. God may bless you with a greater income; I've seen him do that in many people's lives. He may bless you by lowering your expenses. I've seen people step across the line of faith and begin to tithe and God miraculously lowered expenses. It may be through making your possessions last longer than they physically should. This is one of the ways my wife, Kathy, and I have seen God work in our lives. He has blessed us with things we dreamed of but never prayed for, and increased the lifespan of many necessary items. We always said we wanted to spend our 25th anniversary in Hawaii; when it came time to celebrate it Hawaii was not within our budget. We were content with celebrating by going out to dinner at a local restaurant. A family in our church, with no idea about our dream, offered to let us use their condo in Maui for few weeks when they heard we were celebrating 25 years. We were grateful to God our loving Heavenly Father, but not too surprised because it's often been His way with us. I don't know how God will pour out His blessings on you as you live in His financial plan through tithing. But I know He will because He promised it in His Word, and He always keeps His Word. God says this about His own character: "*In my holiness I cannot lie*" (Psalms 89:35b).

A BOSTON 5'10" GRAND

Let me illustrate God's blessings beyond our needs as we are faithful to trust Him through tithe and offerings. I am a musician; I play the piano. When I went to college as a teenager I had scholarships in both art and music. At the time I pursued music with a passion. There was nothing more wonderful to me than sitting down at a quality piano and spend time worshiping God.

During a season of college my oldest sister, Julie, worked for a couple living in a mansion. They provided her an apartment over one of their garages; it was fairly close to where I attended college. They had a music room with a full size Steinway and Sons concert grand piano. In our current market it would cost about $100,000 dollars. She made arrangements with the owners for me to play that beautiful instrument when I visited her. It was an honor and a privilege. As I sat and played, I could see through the wall of windows into the woods overlooking a pond. It was perfect, I loved it. From that moment on I wanted a grand piano, not a Steinway necessarily; I don't live in that world. At one point I thought seriously about going into debt to own one, God kept me from it. As the years passed the love for worshiping in solitude while playing the piano never waned, nor did the desire for a grand piano.

I had a pastor friend whose church, in an effort to be more contemporary, quit using their grand piano. It was actually in a big storage closet off to the side of their main auditorium. I asked him if he would ever sell it. He was uncertain what the donors of the piano would think about the idea. I told him if they ever decided to sell, let me know first and I made an offer. My offer was what I could afford, it was only 25% of the piano's worth. Over the years I periodically reminded him of my desire to purchase the piano. Then one day, because of difficult circumstances, they had to close the doors of the church. The remaining congregation would join him in planting a new church in our community. He told me they needed money to make repairs on the building in order to sell it. Would I still be willing to buy the piano for the amount I had offered years ago? My offer was the exact amount they needed for the repairs. I knew God was blessing me and I got to be a part of helping another church launch in our community through this deal.

Today if you walk into our home you will see a black Boston 5'10" grand piano sitting in our living room. Interestingly, the piano I had when I married my wife Kathy was a Boston studio piano; I loved that piano. I did a lot of worshiping and song writing at that piano. We had to sell it to cover the need of our young family. I never regretted it; my wife and kids are such an amazing blessing. But I always hoped one day to sit at a piano of quality, similar to the one where my sister worked and lived, and just get lost in worship. If you don't know pianos, the Boston grand piano was designed by Steinway and Sons for another piano maker. It's one of God's many blessings in my life. When people come into our home I am often asked if I will play for them or lead them in a song of worship. I'm flattered they ask but kindly decline or redirect the conversation. At this point in my life, sitting at the piano and worshiping God is just for me and Him. There are times when I feel a prompting of God asking me if I'm willing to sell the piano or give it away, the answer is always yes. Like every blessing in my life it's His to do with whatever He wants. I sometimes think it would be awesome if God used me to move that Boston into the hands of another church who would be blessed and use it for His glory. Because that is how He works. He is just looking to His kids to be faithful with His stuff, and to move it around to where it's needed to advance His kingdom. What a privilege to be a part of His grand plans! In the meantime, I will enjoy His piano.

TAKE THE CHALLENGE

If you're reading this and don't attend the church I pastor, I can't offer you the tithe challenge. I wish I could because I have seen exponential spiritual growth in every person that takes it and follows through. Living within God's financial system of tithing is essential for your spiritual growth. It is a way of expressing your thanks and love to Him. Investing in eternity through

> You will never be able to out-give God.

His plan is the greatest investment you will ever make in this life; and you will never be able to out-give Him.

If you are new to this part of your faith journey as a follower of Jesus, the whole idea probably scares you a little, or a lot! The cost may seem too far out there for you to even imagine. As in all things, there is a cost for stepping out in faith and trusting God. I love the words of David when he went to sacrifice to God. "*I will not present burnt offerings to the Lord my God that have cost me nothing*" (2 Samuel 24:24b). He understood that God deserves our very best. He understood to give to God out of our leftovers is an insult to the God of the universe who loves us so much He sent His Son to die for our sins on the cross.

EPILOGUE

Here are a few simple thoughts in conclusion. First, I want you to know no matter what you decide to do in regard to trusting God with your finances, Kathy and I remain committed to God's financial system. He has proven Himself true to us, it has been a life changing journey. There are moments we struggle financially and are tempted, and then we remember it's all His. He is truly Lord of the fries, and so we push through to give even more in those moments. Second, if you are a follower of Jesus and are married to a spouse who objects to your giving to God, walk circumspectly. Your spouse's salvation falls under the more important things that Jesus was speaking of in Matthew 23:23b: "*For you are careful to tithe even the tiniest income from your herb gardens, but you ignore the more important aspects of the law—justice, mercy, and faith. You should tithe, yes, but do not neglect the more important things.*" God doesn't need your fries, what He wants is what they represent, your heart.

The number one key to giving is first give yourself to Him, "*...their first action was to give themselves to the Lord...*" (2 Corinthians 8:5b). Your faith and relationship with God are precious commodities to Him, after all He made the first move toward you. "*But God showed his great love for us by sending Christ to die for us while we were still sinners*" (Romans 5:8). He will bless you on this journey as you commit your finances into His hands. "*Commit everything you do to the Lord. Trust him, and he will help you*" (Psalms 37:5). You are not on your own. He will help you. He will empower you. My passion and prayer is for God to stir up your faith to trust Him as your provider and beyond, that you would be able to trust Him as your loving Heavenly Father so completely, through Jesus, and experience the fullness of His love.

ACKNOWLEDGEMENTS

Thank you to the leaders and team at Alive Church who passionately pursue the heart of the Father. And to the many people who call Alive Church home both in person and online. You continually challenge my thinking and sharpen my skills as one who is committed to creatively communicating the Gospel.

Thank you to the hands-on team of this book. Kristi, my daughter and assistant, in her strategic leadership as project manager. To my sister and brother-in-law, Julie and Jim Joiner. You are more than just editors, you breathe life into the words of these pages. Your commitment to communicating the message found here goes beyond expectation.

Thank you to my family. To all four of my kids for your willingness and openness to share your story and our relationship to help others. I am a very proud papa! To my wife Kathy, I can't imagine this journey without you. Your "can-do" attitude, love, support and thinking add more value to my life than I could ever hope to add to others.

Thank You, Jesus. I am honored to do what You have me doing as a pastor and author. I believe the words of these pages with all my heart and ask for Your strength and wisdom to live them in a greater way every day. I trust You as my provider in all things.

ABOUT THE AUTHOR

Dr. Jeffrey Allen Love is a communicator committed to adding value through creatively communicating the Gospel. His writing and messages impact others by releasing their God-given potential. He is the lead/teaching pastor at Alive church in Tucson, Arizona. He is the author of *Life Palette: God created a masterpiece...and it's you!* He and his wife Kathy have four children and one grandchild. Healthy growing relationships with God the Father, family and friends is a high life priority for them.

CONNECT WITH

DR. JEFFREY ALLEN LOVE

- Blog: lordofthefriesbook.com

- Face Book: lifepalettebook & jeffreyallenlove

- Twitter: artisanjefflove

- Check out his teachings: Alivechurch.com

Watch For

Alive Church

LIFE TRANSFORMATION BIBLE

with Dr. Jeffrey Allen Love

Coming
Easter 2017

PASTORS AND CHURCHES

Be sure to check out alivechurch.com and lordofthefriesbook.com for free resources!

1. Sermons outlines from *Lord Of The Fries*

2. Video sermon illustration to use during a *Lord Of The Fries* series

3. Downloadable small group material

4. Bulk discounts for books

Speaking inquires: jeff@alivechurch.com

LIFE PALETTE
GOD MADE A MASTERPIECE...AND IT'S YOU!

DR. JEFFREY ALLEN LOVE

Adam Colwell's writeworks

Tucson, AZ
in cooperation with 2911 publishing